The Listening God

The Listening God

Miriam Pollard, OCSO

With illustrations by the author.

Michael Glazier
Wilmington, Delaware

First published in 1989 by Michael Glazier, Inc., 1935 West Fourth St., Wilmington, Delaware, 19805. ©1989 by Michael Glazier, Inc. All rights reserved. Printed in the United States of America.

International Standard Book Number: 0-89453-767-9
Library of Congress Catalog Card Number: 88-27232

Library of Congress Cataloging-in-Publication Data
Pollard, Miriam.
    The listening God / Miriam Pollard.
    p.   cm.
    ISBN 0-89453-767-9
    1. Meditations.   I. Title.
BX2182.2.P57   1989   88-27232
248.4--dc19   CIP

Typography by Edith Warren, Angela Meades.
Designed by Maureen Daney.

Contents

Fore-thoughts
7

Listening
15

A Year Later
103

*For Mother Agnes
with grateful love.
All her paths are peace.*

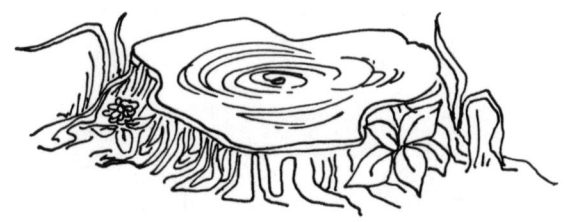

fore-thoughts

Yes, I know.

It's we who should be listening. And we really want to. We know we can be so agitated by what seems to be wrong with everything that the tranquil voice of God can't get a word in edgewise.

We'd like to make a space into which God can come and have his say. But all that's wrong with the way things are keeps provoking our emotions to complaint, resentment, and the unrelenting desire for a change of circumstance. No space is left to listen in, no inner peace in which the word of God can root. And prayer can become either a dreary duty or a terrible struggle to calm down.

But maybe we haven't begun in the right place. It's at least possible that some of us ought to begin by speaking. We can then learn a comforting paradox: the God to whom we want to listen is also the God who often speaks by listening to us.

How?

Most of us already know the basic principles of faith, truths which, when drawn up into the problem areas of our lives, can help us stop fighting the daily run of commonplace disaster. The listening heart of God draws out of us this wisdom he has been sowing in us all along. We need to speak to him in order to know what we already think we know, and in order to hold out the classical thorn in the paw.

The great truths, those to which we must return over

and over, and with personal urgency, are few, large, and simple. We often feel we know them because we've heard them, lived with them, and dismissed them as cliches. We think we must search for something new and wonderful, and until we find it, must remain the victim of our vast and noisy discomfort.

Usually, without realizing it, we already have everything we need, and talking the matter out with God matches a familiar principle with a current problem to reveal both principle and problem as the soil of an immense love. Often then we reach a fuller possibility for inner quiet, one that reaches more deeply into the personality than a mere cessation of noise. We can't always get a day of recollection when we most need one, but we can always speak into the warm, receptive silence of a God whose very being is all the space we need. There we can talk ourselves into the stillness of knowing we are loved, protected, and listened to.

This book is that kind of thing. I am helped myself by writing out my struggles to live by faith and common sense. I find this quieting, and if in the writing process, I can stop and sit in wordless prayer, I do. It's that simple.

These reflections talk about the common things I see around me, things perhaps too common to be talked about; and expose at the same time, a person also perhaps too common to be talked about except that people tell me they are reassured to know they don't have to be extraordinary to be valuable. They will see themselves in these meditations—creatures like me of habit and emotion, predictably inclined to stop short at appearances, get mad at frustrations and ignore abundant evidences of God's creative love.

They may learn as I have, that God has patience with a determination to sulk, but that he takes a dim view of the talent for brewing hurricanes in teapots. The world, he tells me, is far more beautiful than I am inclined to give it credit for. He wants to give me spunk enough to see that it is beautiful in spite of all we do (and all I do) to mess it up.

For even when civilization has substituted concrete for hayfields, it cannot eliminate sun and shadow, rain on window glass, or the silent harmony of lines and planes. I have read of a photographer who teaches her art to inner city children. For the first time, they have learned to see beauty. Even our cruelty to one another cannot send into exile the God of beautiful things.

But there is more. A circumstance may not be beautiful; it may scrape and scour, and all we want is for it not to be. That's when we have to look again at everything we think we know just because we stored it long ago in some mental closet.

Does God love me?

Do I believe this?

Has he the power, the desire, and the ingenuity to bring good out of evil, or am I oppressed by feeling that the world he made has painted him into a corner?

Do the Incarnation and the journey of Christ through life into death and out the other side have a real relationship to the difficulty that presently weighs my spirit?

These are the great simplicities of life that I may "believe" and yet need to wrestle with in the concrete situation God has permitted to grow up around me.

These meditations are conversations with the God who listens, not resignedly but eagerly, to each of us who wants to love and to accept his love, to listen and be heard. If I do not speak a great deal about the monumental sorrows of existence, I hope there is some help here for the person who wants to see and enjoy its smaller glories and find meaning instead of discontent in the ordinary scrapes and bruises of today.

You will appreciate a couple of explanations. What, for instance, are hermit days? The monastic tradition to which I belong and the tradition of my own monastery in particular put a strong emphasis on community. We grow through teamwork and a quiet, but fairly busy kind of communal living. So about three times a month we get a day for being hermits—community-hermits, one might say. This is one way of renewing the solitude in which our love and understanding of one another is rooted.

Another explanation. Someone who read these meditations asked if all my mornings were bad. Not at all. I was, at the time they were being written, engaged in conflict with a machine. I wanted to win, not most but all the time, and that monster of iron, copper and steel taught me wonderful things about God and myself. I'm still not sure who won the fight, but I came off richer and happier—and maybe, if possible, a little humbler.

The postcript to the book was written about a year after the main body of the reflections, during a brief period of filling in for the novice-mistresss who had to attend a workshop. Everyone should go back to the beginning now and then. It's encouraging to know that after thirty years, you've begun to understand what you were taught there.

As a cautionary note, I would add that this type of reflection is a prayer method, a way of absorbing truth into the joys and stresses of life. It does not substitute for the view from outside provided by a spiritual advisor or a perceptive friend. We need to check our perspective at least now and then, against the more objective outlook of someone looking on.

LISTENING

Fog

This view has pines, a valley, and distant hills. Its pines are all there is today, for the valley and hills are fogged out, a long charcoal smudge at the base of the grey sky. Swallows dash off into the fog. Swallows will dash off into anything.

Yesterday I read that now and then we should ask of common things, "What would I feel about this if I knew I were never to see it again?" So I have spent the morning of this hermit day inspecting a variety of natural objects and have concluded that if I were to die tonight, today would have justified the gift of life. That sounds extravagant. It also sounds self-important. The world probably does not need my homage, but I am glad to have given it. I wish I could feel less guilty about striking a pose at its expense: the nature-lover getting in the way of the view.

This bench is the end of my travels. I have brought a lunch and will eat it here unless I get rained inside. From here you catch the sound of cars off on 121. A car on the highway sounds like the whoosh that a stiff wind gets out of the trees. I hear thunder also, and will certainly be rained on.

A view is like the future. The future is many things. It is a continuation of the life we know, but also the incomprehensible afterwards—and, as a matter of fact, both together with a lot else thrown in. We shouldn't fear it. It is beautiful and veiled, like the foggy valley. Swallows do not fear it. Why should I?

Tomorrow may be more of yesterday or more of last Tuesday which was dreadful. But still it is most like this view—stately, tantalizing, right. We determine so much of our own future; we make a lot of it for ourselves by finding or not finding what it hides, by accepting or rejecting the present. There is so much to discover in both places.

Wild geese. I only hear them. Maybe they are on a pond, or in somebody's cornfield. Maybe they aren't geese at all: my ear could trick me. They might be dogs very far away. Beside me a pine leans against another, relic of a hurricane. Half its roots are sufficient for it. The other half, pulled up, still provides a surface for growing plants. Nature finds a use for everything.

God has made so much beauty. "Life is so generous a giver." Want tomorrow.

Answered

Silence has advantages—not always the ones you read about in books, but new ones, fine ones, advantages you can't be told about but can only discover for yourself in an experience of need.

I've been reading a book about the sea, a book with pictures. No one can really photograph the sea, for a photo stills its movement. But a photo can at least suggest. Of all nature, the sea is most like God. My father was a sailor, and my earliest memories are of water, ships, and horizons. Later came hurricanes.

Who wants to talk in the presence of the sea? Who wants to carry on the compulsive effort to establish in someone else's perception a satisfying projection of yourself?

It isn't necessary there to build an image, hardly necessary to exist at all. Or rather and better, you receive the reassuring surprise that to forget about your own existence in attending to something else is to find it for the first time.

Everything you could say is washed out of your head by the movement of water and the sea's insistent simplicity. You are wholly happy in losing the desire to speak. It has been taken from you.

Angels have a bad press. I don't like them much myself. I have a hard time dropping the imagery in which history has tried to cope with them. But they

wouldn't bother me if they could be thought about as this silence over the face of the sea. The sea of course is never quiet; it's always making sound. The quiet that attends it is a refusal to interfere, a vast unwillingness to defend, construct, or get nervous about whatever it is you want to be.

Words are a collection, but the sea makes you whole. Words are a plea, but here you have been answered.

◇

Benny

When he died, I remembered.

One evening before I came to the monastery, we went to hear Benny Goodman. Massachusetts had Blue Laws then and he had to quit at midnight. We all stood. Nobody wanted to dance or maybe there was no room. Occasionally the crowd yelled. "'Sing, Sing, Sing', Benny!" He saved it for last.

He was so quiet, so understated, in a blue alpaca suit. Like anyone. But the clarinet was something else. Where do you draw a line between a personality and its skill, between what you are and what your art discovers?

He played only jazz that night, though he was as good at classical. His classical instructor had told him he'd been lipping improperly all his life so he learned to do it right. His humility rearranged the callouses on his lips.

What's it like to be a man like that, someone who walks in like anyone and stands unagitated in a ruckus of applause, yet travels regularly into a mystery much greater than the sum of all the thoughts and emotions he can account for on any given day; someone with access to a world much larger than the man who opens its door?

I do not grieve. Anyone who spent his life like that is comfortable in the place he's come to. He left a Brahms quintet on his music stand, open for tomorrow. Tomorrow changed his plans. What he knew, he now knows better.

I want to say thank you—thank you because I remember "Sing, Sing, Sing", and it is more than an interpretation of life. It's an excursion into the courage to love it. Life can look like a garbage can sometimes, but it doesn't have to be one. Even the worst mismanagement of possibility gets eventually to its midnight. And no one has to quit and go home. Silence—this time the chill and unresponsive silence of negation—doesn't have to smother the bandstand when the clock strikes twelve. There's an ending but it's not that, a meaning but not that one.

"Sing, Sing, Sing", Benny.

Yeah.

On the Bias

Someone put a clay pot of petunias on a stump outside the Chapter Room. They are scraggly and ought to have been pinched back to encourage bushiness. They lack perfection, but they have something else—the spice of imperfection, of a good try that missed and doesn't mind.

Formal gardens in parks or around wealthy homes could have their pictures taken for the cover of *Horticulture*. Even when ours look well, they aren't that kind of thing. A concrete urn of Patience Plant, for instance, is standing on the bias with paint chipped off its base.

Our flowers sometimes need a hair dresser. They are at home with us—the day lilies with their unmessable yellow dignity, the scrawny geraniums, morning glories all foliage and red spider, the sleek and fragrant roses. Our successes, near misses and flops do not feel the need to apologize, to fit an artificial standard. They are cheerful and reassuring.

Out by the statue in the cemetery, half an arborvitae has gone brown. It is celebrating its independence from the need to be a glossy magazine cover. The world has got out from under the techniques of management and is enjoying itself.

Perhaps I should celebrate my own independence from the responsibility for running it. Maybe I could let it be itself for a change; maybe I could enjoy its spunkiness.

The house inside can be like this as well; people can be; life in general. There is usually a tile loose on the floor, usually a tile loose in someone's personality—clank. Let me enjoy loose tiles and flowering weeds, vagaries of character that save a community from insipidity, that give it crunch.

Save me from putting up with people. Give me a taste for the distinctive, the dandelion. Give me delight in what is not myself, in all that climbs my walls with ivy hands and cracks the rock.

Give me patience with my own peculiarities, for no one else's are so hard to appreciate, so impossible to like.

P.S. I'm sorry to say that this year the pot of petunias (and a lot else) has been replaced by pots of begonias. Begonias seem to resist bugs, drought, stretching, and imperfection in general. They're hard to live with but God made them, and I will have to figure out a way to think about them. Someday.

The City

Sun against the bookcase casts a shadow-city on the wall behind. It builds high-rises, steeples, a church with two domes.

I know that the city is not really a shadow. I cannot slap an answer on it and go away. (When the sun shifts, there will be no more city.) I carry around the mystery of the city's poor, of people with no possibility.

I do not know why the healing I can give depends on my attentiveness to gratitude, or why it is my call to labor at building joy. Despair would seem to be more congruent. Shouldn't my day go into mourning for the dying cities of the world?

There is joy and there is joy, of course. I'm not talking about the kind that grows like fungus on the rot of human desire, that spreads its table linen on the wretchedness of those who have no food.

I mean the simplicity of doing what one is able to do, and in the process laying one's hands in those of him who is the city's love and the city's cry. Christ of the city, I pour on your lacerated body the wine and oil of a refusal to sulk over my own petty concerns, over not having got what I want, not being able to be what I want.

Consider the dark and littered streets of my heart. I give you my private metropolis to walk around in, my slums so you can sit on their curbs. Give me the courage to trust in your astringent joy.

Being poor is to be without importance, without respect or independence. It is—almost—to be without existence. In choosing to accept a worthlessness that other people have no choice about, in letting slip my assortment of pretensions, my stock of affirmation, I can be where they are, in reality if not in geography.

There is more. Back alleys and gin, vermin and hunger and the stench of rotting hope are not the end. There is more. Not to be is not the end at all. There is more.

Wombats Sleep by Day

I just read an article about a man who runs a homemade zoo in Australia.

Lord, I like your wombats. Australia has interesting animals. You don't find wombats in Boston. (I doubt that even the Franklin Park Zoo has any.) They sleep all day. This is an agreeable state of affairs. The article said they look like a cross between a ground hog and a sack of meal. I've seen a picture. They do.

(This man keeps Tasmanian Devils also. You can't make friends with a Tasmanian Devil. It's a wonder they can make friends with each other.)

God, how lavish you are with curiosities and amiable creatures. One has only to consider dolphins, whippets, hedgehogs, killdeer, and certain cats—not to mention otters and the ponderous self-possession of the whale.

Oh God, I am very sorry. I hardly ever notice. It's as if you were trying to engage me in a conversation and I were absorbed in research on the reconstruction of antique sewage systems. It's as if you were saying, "Sewage has its place, but you'd be better fitted to deal with it if you spent some time deciphering my marginal notes to the world's appraisal of itself."

Indeed.

Giving

I'm ashamed.

Why should I hurt over such a trifle. Why should I hurt at all? I have so much; I wallow in gifts—food, shelter, people, the opportunity to pray. I am a modest-sized hippo in a river of grace and comfort, sloshing in agreeable mud.

I open the crucifixion account. Now *there* was something to complain about. That was respectable pain. Nothing was missing to make it universally awful. I ponder it with respect. I try to put my own trifle in a back pocket but it won't stay sat on. You might as well try to sit on a lobster. It wants to be felt and minded and paid attention to.

"My friend," says the hunk of flesh bleeding above me, baking in the hot minutes of his allotted hour. "I'll take it. Give it here. I have nothing to do right now."

I'm ashamed. Get back in my pocket, little pain, discordant restlessness. Look, Lord, if it were an appreciable drama, you'd be welcome to it. Bad enough to suffer from it without letting you take it on, mess up the fine exigency of your own predicament. Never.

"But what I am I here for? I hang between time and infinity, measuring the distance between freedom and the servitude of small compensations. Your pain is the wound left by losing such a compensation. You will never be free if you hug the pain to yourself as you did the possession you have lost. Give me your trifle. I want to love it; I want to get it out of your back pocket, out in the air where it won't go bad. I want it to be mine. I want to gather it in and give it a certain proportionate glory."

Ok, I give it up. If it will comfort you, I'll part with it, share it, turn it over. Perhaps then my hurt will be no longer alien to you, no longer your oppressor but yourself. My trifle—here it is. I won't hog its unimportance. You take it and keep it. Carry it on your bloodstream, let it heave on your breath.

That's not quite all though, is it? What is my discontent,

what is my hurt (large or small) but a more considerable discontent at what I have to be?

"Give me the self you do not want to be. Give it here. Let it stop squirming and be still, held in the self I am. Let it sleep my sleep and wake my waking."

Faces

Richard Avedon's photograph is as real as Dorothy Day herself, and even his famous cock-eyed composition expresses the integrity of her disorganization. I wish I had seen every print he made of her. Did he ever get a chance at Eleanor Roosevelt? Flannery O'Connor? Probably not. It's too bad. I list to myself the faces I would want him to explore.

I remember a column—it was a meditation actually—by Melvin Maddocks, explaining the superiority of the older face. The camera could linger for long minutes, he said, on the face of Katherine Hepburn, of Henry Fonda. It had something worthwhile to do there.

The Metropolitan Museum has compiled a volume of photos which it calls *The Face of Lincoln*. You can buy it for some incredible price, and if you do, you would be buying a pilgrimage to the roots of human destiny. Every concept, every explanation comes to a respectful halt before that face and motions you to go on alone.

(Maybe you can get it at a public library. I would not want its advantages confined to the people who can pay incredible prices.)

Let us give thanks for faces made wonderful by people who have not quite got along with life but lived it anyway, who have carried unanswerable questions and unbearable weights and still have what it takes to crack a joke. Let us construct a liturgy of eyes and hands, skin stretched over noses, creased cheeks, and feet in old shoes.

It's hard to imagine the resurrection of the body. The heart rebels at losing faces that have lived, and getting in exchange bland expanses of ungraven cheek. Maybe it will all be in the eyes. At any rate, we are not now in danger of restoration. We can praise the topography of experience.

Here is beauty left behind by simple joys. Here is beauty not destroyed but wrought by inclement circumstance, plans that didn't work, and insubstantial loves.

The work of creation can issue in something other but not less than Eden. Give us faces like mountains, like oak trunks and plowed land; faces shaped by wind and unpredictable waters. Give us rest in their solitudes and peace in the tenacity of their inconsistencies.

Let us praise people, not worn but formed by time's refusal to cooperate, faces eroded to a beauty we get a taste for after a certain amount of life.

The Way Things Are

A couple of hawks.
Hawks must do a lot of flying for the fun of it. They can't always be hunting. The call of a hawk is quite a comedown. Their flight is beautiful; their sound is awful. Maybe they should just fly and keep their mouths shut.

I wait. The hawks have gone away and perhaps nothing else will come. One never knows. Cicadas and wind keep the afternoon going. Summer maintains a running commentary on the state of things.

I disconnect my drive to get things done, tidied up, written, taken care of. How much life is waiting for me? I need not press against the end of it.

Something is happening—a small flock of birds is leaving town. I continue to wait after they have gone. Thinking about God makes me tense. I wish I knew why. This week has not been so bad. I can't say that I carried it gracefully but I kept trying to do better. That's a good week. At least my head tells me so.

Clouds, dark clouds. Bother. Wind. More rain is coming.

The police helicopter. Not nearly as interesting as hawks. God makes things better than we do, with the possible exception of sailing ships.

I suppose the week has not been good. I didn't want to fail, and failure made me feel worthless and I got mad. I don't know how to bring God into it, or to deal with him

when I have to stop and realize he has got in anyway, in spite of me.

What kind of prayer is this: The world is going to fall down and bury me, I hate the people over whose feet I stumble in my compulsion to perform without a hitch. I suffer more from anxiety over what will never happen than over the things that do.

But the world out here is good, clouds notwithstanding. Gentle. I stop trying to solve God and life and anything at all. The way things are has its advantages. I will go and make my hermit lunch.

Green Shoulders

I do not have to offer my day to God. My day *is* God. My day is not a succession of events, pleasures, irritations, satisfactions, and frustrations. It is not successes and mistakes, opportunities and dead-ends. It is God.

He is a sea drinking the undistinguished trickles of my life, heaving them outwards toward its horizon. My day is not me accepting God but God accepting me, enjoying me, travelling off with me upon the green shoulders of his reliable tide.

My little frustrations are the mighty adventures of God. My pleasures are tidepools shimmering with his creative intent.

The Squirrel

A squirrel just heisted an ear of corn from the garden and is eating it on the branch of a tree. Obviously this is not its first theft. It has scattered a history of corn leaves and chewed cobs throughout the long grass.

A flock of crows cruises the hayfield. My morning—a very bad morning littered with bad decisions—melts into one o'clock of a soft fall day. Corn leaves are hanging from a branch of rusty leaves. That squirrel gets around.

You can't just bury a morning like that, or rather you shouldn't. You are angry with it, you hate it, you hate yourself. But you must not go away in a hate. You must bless the pieces of the morning, try to understand your hatred, and maybe bless that too.

I think of prison camps, ghettos, mental hospitals. My small morning isn't so bad. Yet that's not the answer. My squirrel is cursing and lashing his tail. Squirrel, you remind me of myself. Dragonflies are courting on the doorstep of death. Oh squirrel, *please*. Don't squeak so.

What does one hate in such a morning? I poke around in it with a mental finger. The flesh is sore but why? The wounds were given, not by circumstance, not by an objective force which levelled its artillery at me from outside myself, but by me. My reaction to circumstance and then my reaction to my reaction were the agents of a lousy morning.

But what good is it to realize there's nothing there to hate? It doesn't turn off the pain or the regret.

It does something. It has to. Knowing that emotion has nothingness as its object has to do something to you. You have to ask the question, "Is this nothing hiding anything inside itself?" You know the answer, or you know it as theory. The question really is, "Do you believe it enough to let it affect the way you are reacting?"

Inside the nothingness, there is—calm, resolute, and of absolute reliability—a Providence that says, "Leave the pieces where they fell and let me make what I want of them. Are you determined to lose the morning twice? Once by messing it up and once by refusing to make peace with the mess, refusing to let me put it back together my way?"

Give thanks.

Bless the morning, the noon, the squirrel, tomorrow, yesterday and every hour that lies in pieces on the ground. Anyone who can put dry bones back together is capable of raising up a broken morning.

Son of man, these bones will live.

Amen.

The Day After Yesterday

In twenty minutes I have to go to do dishes. Meanwhile, it is more or less noon on a windy summer day. Someone has painted six wicker chairs a soft lemon yellow, without mending them, and they sit over there getting dry.

Stalks of brown grass bend over my feet and I consider the south view. Its valley is almost too narrow to see. You only see the tops of its trees before they start climbing the hill. A black butterfly and two swallows. The hill is striped with sun and shadow, the wind smells warm.

Yesterday has dissolved. Just as well. Who wants it? But it seemed so solid then, so inevitable and permanent. A little sun has erased it, a little wind. Maybe it's so with life in general. Sun lies pleasantly on my toes. The air is good enough to drink.

One benefit of being here is that you do not have to oblige yourself to be an individual. It's as good as growing roots and leaves like everything else around. You wiggle contented branches.

Or maybe contentment itself is something you don't need at all, something a great deal less than what you have.

Forested

It's a small thing to accept not getting what you want.

It's another and much harder thing to accept your inability to get the Redemption all figured out; harder to yield oneself to the confusion of being saved, now in the concrete. I do not belittle the intellect. It does a job. It proceeds to a point. But it does not outstrip the heart. It does not go so far.

And we are left so unattended, so without explanation, so forested and without a compass. We try to stop the running off in all directions of a brain goaded by the inconvenience of having more to do than it was made to handle. We try to soothe its poison ivy and coax it back. Stay put. Tie yourself to a tree and shut up. Stop trying to explain everything.

Let me accept the inexplicable without clamor—the great facts of need, want, longing, evil, self-serving, freedom, joy, and helplessness. Let me face gratuity without trying to figure it out of existence.

Let me stop.

Nothing will be gained at this point by pressing the understanding beyond its capacity. Let the head rest, the famous and articulate brain. Let the heart hang up a sign in several languages, "Shhhh!" Give me prayer that doesn't move, that soaks, that sits because it knows there isn't any use in moving any more, that stops the fuss.

Let me pray a prayer that gives itself over to not understanding.

Let me plunk myself under a tree and agree to stop exploring—above all, stop trying to get out of the woods. Getting out of them is not the primary purpose of trees.

◊

Green

I'm very grateful for the color green. If there had to be so much of anything, best it be green.

But I have never before thought to accept it as my own personal gift. I have walked through it, on it, under it. I have enjoyed it, but it has never been my own. That seemed selfish. It was everybody else's too. How could it be special for me?

Lord, today I am sitting on the lawn and everything except the sky is a different shade of green. The wind blows green, the chipping sparrow is spitting little green sounds. Fern wiggles pleasantly under its trees. The world is a present tied up in green wrapping paper, the world is lime sherbet after the heat.

This is my day—all mine. It can be all mine and all everyone else's too because it is distinct and special for each person. I want you to know I like it. I lick the sherbet slowly; I love the world, going around its edges carefully to get it all loved with nothing left out.

I think of all the places where no green comes, the dry and hostile places. I paint them with desire, with concern. Let the green in.

Thank you for lichens, for small spruce hugging the edges of tundra. Thank you for this gentle color in which you have wrapped your world. Thank you for giving it to me.

Today is a green balloon, and I toss it back to you.

Today is a game we play in July.

◇

Portly and I

How often do I sit down and decide to accept the Trinity?

We think of God accepting us. We don't realize he is up a tree unless we accept *him*. He can't do much with the love he has for us until we give him permission to use it. This permission is not so easily given. We slide out of it.

OK, I will try to allow you to love me. I accept. I give you permission to be yourself. It's not that easily said, not that easily meant. It's scarey.

I won't look away from the knowledge you have

given me of what, of who you are: this embarrassing complexity that I can't understand, that—I might say it softly—I am almost bored with. The Trinity. Jesus, Lord Christ, I am not good with abstractions and Trinitarian theology sounds like an abstraction to me.

But the Trinity is not theology. Theology is our clumsy way of trying to figure it out.

I remember that charming image of Portly, the baby otter, curled up asleep between the hooves of Pan in *The Wind in the Willows*. That's how I feel, and I would like to take his place. The Trinity—my being, my life, my answer—is too big for me. It falls down over me and knocks my breath out. If only it had hooves to sleep between, I would be more at home with it.

Of course, maybe it has.

The human brain abstracts. This is useful and gives us a sense of accomplishment. But God does not abstract. Instead, he translates himself into created being. Admittedly, the translation stutters. But it tells you that you are not destined to be imprisoned forever in the negation of what you were made to want.

God translates himself into sunlight, into the plumage of birds, into pine needles and lighted windows in the snow. The Trinity is not a concept on the outskirts of the mind. God dresses himself in dyed garments.

I say yes to the enormity of God. It is the stream-head from which all creation tumbles. I curl up beside Portly and sleep.

Feeding the Jokes

Once upon a time we had a Russian wolfhound. We gave him to a neighbor because he looked incongruous around a barn. (A borzoi has such a delicate appearance, it comes as a surprise to refer to one as "he". But they must be tough. After all, hunting in Siberia is no joke.)

There are also Irish wolfhounds. They look as if they had forgotten to brush their hair when they got up in the morning. I suppose it's natural and they look that way even when they've been groomed. Irish wolfhounds are longer than any other dog. When they stand on their hind legs and put their front paws on your shoulders, they make you feel inferior. If your knees collapse, you feel even more inferior. The problem with wolfhounds, of course, is the food bill.

Our dog eats vegetables. The manuals would be appalled, but she is overweight. Our cats eat vegetables but also mice, chipmunks, and so forth which they sometimes drop at your feet for a gift. One could wish for the peaceable kingdom, but they cannot be convinced of its value.

I have a postcard of a shur dog—that very expensive Chinese breed which looks as if it's going to lose its skin any minute, or as if it has spent its life in the dishpan getting wrinkled. A Sister in San Diego sent the postcard because she figured that if basset hounds helped me pray, a shur would practically do my praying for me.

It's well to ponder these eccentricities of creation when everything gets awful. The awful has a habit of weighing more, sounding louder, and tasting worse than the beautiful and true. The beautiful and true cultivate a certain unobtrusiveness.

Humor—the uncanned, built-in, lithe and unlabored mirth of the way things are—can refresh our taste for the unobtrusive, and mess up our confidence in the infallibility of our own dreary evaluations.

◊

I Want To

What is it that I accept in accepting the gentle, the boring, the contrary, and the routinely beautiful?

What do I accept in the hurt of having my opinions and preferences over-ridden, in the solitude of being left out, the chill of having no roof over my small wants? Or, on the other hand, what do I accept in the peace of fir trees before night, the reliable comfort of birds?

What do I accept in accepting?

God, certainly, and in many ways. I remember the way St. Therese got herself to accept the delay of her Clothing ceremony. She would make a wedding dress. (The beguiling thing about Therese is the way she could turn a childish desire and even a childish image into a mature resolution without even the seams showing.) Her dress would be jewelled with sacrifice, and when she was properly dressed, the bridegroom would turn up. She would do the unnoticed helpful thing and accept the inconsequential snub, and be glad she could.

There's a truth in her satin and seed-pearls. Disagreeable events are not terrible visitations to be offered up, borne with, and stood. They are benefits we can't yet understand.

And the pleasures, the agreeable projects and good books and people who take the sting out of bee-bites—these too must be accepted. It's bad asceticism to ignore the God of the agreeable, sustaining, and beautiful. He is pleased to be thanked.

Still more, what do I accept? An entire world, a healing, a mystery I am too determined to ignore. If I don't believe in my own healing, how can I believe enough in the world's to draw out the saving power of God? Healing depended on faith, back there in Galilee; it still does. "Do you believe that I can do this?" The world depends on confidence.

Let today's hurt heal me.

Let today's joy heal me.

Let my healing travel beyond my own boring diseases. Let my trust embrace friends and unknown people who struggle with the mystery of pain and inadequacy, with the suicide of a child, addictions, divorce, failure, the collapse of what they need to be. Let it worship in the strong, resilient hearts of people who greet each day at the front door and ask it in.

Lord, I believe, or at least I want to. I accept or at least I want to.

◇

Pearls

If pearls weren't so expensive they would serve us well as objects of meditation. But though autumn foliage comes free, pearls cost money.

I dislike what is done to them. A pendent, a string of pearls, a choker of several strands—these I appreciate. But pearls are desecrated by the jeweller, forced into an uneasy relationship with diamonds. They are tossed into a gemmy goulash where their self-possession is diminished or destroyed.

I would like pearls and not curiosities. Let them not be concocted and tormented into foreign shapes. Leave them lustrous, warm and simple. They should be permitted their natural quietude, unviolated by nonsense. Respect their form, and give us the right to worship in their uncluttered presence. Pearls are a silence to the eye, the sea's expression of its own transcendence. Their beauty can still the agitation of untutored expectation. We stop, we pull ourselves out of a dozen fusses, and drop slowly into an affinity with their delicate glory.

We too have something of the pearl within. We need to embrace this cessation of anxiety, stilling the compulsion to rearrange our own and everyone else's environments. We need to rest in the acknowledgement of our own inner likeness to the pearl.

◇

Churches

The liturgy of autumn celebrates the dedication of two churches. A church is more than a building; it is a symbol of the human heart. Words like Incarnation and Redemption re-write themselves in penmanship of brick, stone, wood, glass, steel, and concrete.

"Destroy this sanctuary and in three days I will raise it up. He was speaking of his body, and when he was raised from the dead, his disciples remembered."

You, Lord Christ, you are my church. I like to go into our own church, but I am always in you. Work is not something I do when I am not in church. It is a different kind of sanctuary. I stand at my place at the caramel wrapper and let you build me into yourself. The acceptance of not knowing what next day's caramel or next day's assistance will be, of not seeing yet a slot into which the rest of what I have to do can slip—this is an agreement to let you build my world, my heart.

I depend. I learn the art of receiving, of dropping conditions and calling a truce in the battle with insecurity. I live today deliberately and let tomorrow arrive in its own time.

Insecurity—precariouness, as Dorothy Day used to put it—is the embrace of God. I am held. The lessons extend.

◊

Gifts

The art of acceptance requires more than taking what you get. It requires going out and counting what you don't yet know you have.

There's an art to taking a gift, just as there's an art to taking a compliment. I remember telling one of the drama majors at school how much I liked her performance in the year-end play. Pat would probably be surprised to know that for 35 years I have remembered the graceful simplicity with which she accepted my compliment. Her acceptance invested me with dignity. She taught me that the reception of a compliment can be a spacious act, a spreading of the heart's wings.

Receiving a gift is all of that and more. Some people do not say, "You shouldn't have." They make you glad you did. The ceremony of the gift is an act of consecration, even when it chiefly provides glue for an elaborate social system. Cultures closer to human roots than ours make much of gifts, for something happens between people in the offering and receiving of a gift. Both sides are in a sense, created and established by the act.

Our culture keeps remnants. We give and receive without quite knowing why, and most of what there is to know about the art of gifts is lost on us.

Giving.

Receiving.

How little we know, how casually we attend. Giving comes first; but let's presuppose the gifts for now and look at receptivity.

We don't notice, for one thing. What we are being given is not all that important to us. How often do we measure, for instance, the disparity between the object in a pretty box tied with a ribbon—the book, the compact disc or wide-angle lens—and the common marvels of an ordinary day? How often do we yield to the etiquette of receiving breath, speech, literacy, smiles, consideration?

Isn't it more usual to walk around all day kicking our most important gifts into the weeds at the side of the road? (And weeds, when you have made their acquaintance, are good gifts in themselves.) Once, when a friend came down with bursitis, I looked it up in the dictionary and went away marvelling at all the joints of so many human bodies in the world that work right. There's so much in us that could go wrong and doesn't.

If you know someone for whom breathing is a struggle, you know what a gift it is to take a series of unreflective breaths. Even a common cold will do this for you. But all of life is a series of unreflective somethings or other. We don't pay attention, so we don't accept the gift. We use it but we don't receive it. Or maybe we don't even use it.

A disabled person, for instance, may have less and be using more. The person without legs or sight or speech, without normal breathing or normal joints, can be so intent on all the other gifts of life, even on the advantages of a particular deprivation, that if the "normal" among us could appreciate the difference, we would see that we are the deprived and not they. We have deprived ourselves of the gift of acceptance.

Take weather. Weather is something we walk around in. Or take people—people are something we walk around beside. We can limit them to the few we need or like or have got used to or can't get away from.

Books can be the ones that slide down easiest or fit our professional requirements. Birds are what mess up the library steps, and windows are holes in the walls.

Knowing what is there is part of the craft of receiving it. But knowing isn't everything. A distorted conscience can be a greater obstacle than indifference. The conscience can be warped in two main directions. The first kind of distortion produces a sense of guilt at being happy, a discomfort with comfort, and a distrust of enjoyment. There is no disability more lethal than amputation of enthusiasm. Lethargy is not virtue.

We must live always in a tension between what—of all the goods available—we may legitimately take, and what we should not take (even when a particular good is not a material object). This is a healthy tension and we should not resolve it by jumping off one end into a puddle of self-produced misery.

We can feel that God has allotted us a definite quota of pleasure, peace, contentment, wonder, and even spiritual understanding—this much. Somewhere the books are kept—this much nice, to be balanced off with something awful. If we're greedy now, we'll lose out later on: "Slowly, not too much enjoyment. Life isn't a sunbath. It's serious. It's for—well, for being miserable in, generally speaking. So many people are suffering. It's not fair to enjoy too much. So many people need help. Shouldn't we be suffering for them? Pleasure is like sneaking a drink on a long hot march. You get it over with and continue your plod. Sweat is the point of life."

Or, "Shouldn't I be suffering for my sins? For somebody else's? For my spiritual advancement? Look at the saints." If I reach out for such good things as tease the edges of my determined line of vision, where does that leave me? A bush league centerfielder when the guys with a talent for suffering are hitting the majors? Other people are onto the Purgative Way, and I notice the sunrise, luxuriate in someone's conversation? I'll be left out, religiously speaking.

Or, even more seriously, "I can't have everything. I'm a disciple and the cross is on my brow. The world is full of enticements to stuff I have no right to, and my will is flabby. How can I safely take advantage of the world's abundance?"

Actually, we know the answers, and one of the best is, "Use your head and make choices." Making choices takes more energy than pulling down all the shades and sitting in the dark. We can be just too tired to choose, too used-up to bother. Our hands can grow too heavy to raise and open, and our hearts too weary to want anything but negation. Taking an interest has become too difficult an enterprise.

We are not made for suffering but for joy. Joy is our native land. Under present circumstances, we will get our share of pain, but we are not asked to stroke and cuddle it like a pet cat. We are invited to hold it as lightly as we can and to find in it, at least eventually, a joy whose character differs from the joy we would have had without the pain. A symbol of this is the morning in the prison camp when Corrie Ten Boom saw the sunlight blazing in the remnants of last night's rain. It glittered on the grass, the bushes—and the barbed wire fence.

This joy is not the counterfeit which ducks out on every possibility for discomfort, or pretends it has no mourning to get through, or suppresses emotional reactions to the common run of frustration, refusing to admit its hurt to itself.

It is something else, something altogether else, and part of its composition is the conviction that pleasure is a visitation of God, an explanation of his person, or upon occasion, a good joke to be shared with him.

It is not only good therapy but good religion to notice the bits of beauty, humor, gracefulness, and social comfort which litter even the barest roads of responsibility. We don't have to lunge at every pleasure in sight; we don't even have to leave the road. God meets us there in small beauties and inconsequential delights. He coaxes our laughter at the incongruity of our self-determination.

The point is harmony. We choose within the area of our responsibility; we do not abandon the responsibility for the sake of discordant pleasure, something which in itself may be agreeable but which disturbs the fundamental balance of our personality and commitments.

But there is more to joy than the grateful acceptance of pleasure. The relationship with God can be difficult; it is not an escape hatch from the bother of being human. But it can also provide solid reassurance that passing trials are passing after all, and that they have meaning. It can seed the ground of trouble with companionship and a mysterious growth.

My father used to have the phrase, "warped out of the true." He got it from his profession, and I like it. A conscience can be warped out of the true. The other main bulge in one's attitude toward pleasure is the "Gobble it all down" warp.

It's one of those things. If we've never learned—or forgotten how—to receive and enjoy, we will gobble and grab. If we have never been helped to see beautiful experiences as a form of communion with God, as a celebration of our own dignity, we consume without discrimination. The pleasure caters, not to a whole human person, but to a dislocated appetite. If we knew more about acceptance, about the truly human art of enjoyment, we would be in much less danger of being seduced from the routes of our responsiblity and devoured by what we devour.

The grateful acceptance of a single common gift, one offered in the daily round of our commitment and compatible with our human dignity, can fill and refresh us so completely that we are no longer torn and tortured by desire for goods which conflict with both dignity and commitment. Or at least these desires can be moderated and understood in the context of a struggle to be faithful to a greater good, a more deeply personal fulfilment.

If only we didn't violate the small beauties of the day, but picked them up, savored and cherished them. If only we gave each one a space in which to root, grow, and establish permanence in memory and prayer. Multiplicity is not the condition for enjoyment, but respect.

Why do we nibble at our pleasures, crumbling the remains and tossing them away with one hand while with the other we reach for one more pleasant stimulation?

◊

Candy Corn

You keep telling me you will take care of things.

Every time I turn around you promise to mind me. It's getting eerie. Never before has this happened with such unabated consistency.

I am making a list of catastrophes to which I responded with anger, pain, or despair; a list also of possible devastations which never happened but which I feared so much that my anxiety made them more real than actual occurrences. The catastrophes have all thrown off their Halloween masks and show freckle faces in search of candy corn. The fears created unnecessary suffering; and several casual wishes came unexpectedly true.

The world is not what I had feared at all. Even the genuinely hard things, when they did turn up, have been both rich and bearable. I do not say there is nothing terrible in life, but that the cross you send is not like the cross I anticipate, the cross manufactured by my anticipation. A determination to be unhappy is not Christian detachment but its opposite.

Faith, Lord, means believing in your cock-eyed efficiency, being alert to your sleight-of-hand, catching the punch lines. And prayer is what—respect for the mystery of how things will turn out? Technique can be the craft of crediting you with good intentions and the power to accomplish them. Maturity is a growing acquaintance with you who mind the store while I'm away.

◊

Turning Off Time

A grey velvet bug has fallen asleep on the plastic pillow I am using for a desk. Cicadas and crickets who survived the cold of last week pack the air with hums and squeaks. A small amount of foliage has turned. Short clumps of maple beside me—short from a fire that turned them from trees into bushes—are producing yellow leaves with red spots, green leaves with red spots, or green and yellow leaves with (what do you know) red spots.

Blackberry foliage has begun to redden. Blackberry's turn is exceedingly dramatic, because its colors are not brilliant but intense and dark. It has much personality.

There's a lot of sky with nothing in it—grey sky that might melt any minute or then again might not. This morning I walked the woods until the fog changed to a drizzle and then to moderate rain. Crawling under a pine, I holed up for an hour, listening to drops slap the neighboring leaves and to the peeps of invisible birds. The fallen leaves were warm and soft to sit on, and I could lean against a low springy branch. Part of that world had also turned color; leaves dropped regularly without sound. The soundlessness of falling leaves is very comforting. I felt like a groundhog on the front porch of its burrow, considering its prospects.

Fern has gone to tan—no excitement there. Beeches are finest and take longest. First they turn yellow but that is not the end of it. I have taken note of places to visit when they have deepened to butterscotch and brown.

To think that all this is only a shadow of the world inside oneself. I think of the Entrance Song to Our Lady's Mass: "He whom the whole world cannot enclose shut himself into your womb and became man." So for all of us.

Today I have tried to disconnect wires leading to absurd preoccupations. I turn off time and accept instead the rhythm of a year curling up for a nap. I have a quarrel with time. There are two sides to it. I can take time's side or mine, and feel entirely justified either way. Today, let us look at mine.

Who made time? God didn't. He never made a clock. He made seasons, mornings, noons, and nights. It's we who jammed his good ideas into a row of mental cages and locked their doors. He didn't make hours or appointment calendars. We did. He puts up with a lot.

It's wise to step out of time occasionally, to sit in a season instead of a cage and tell yourself that all this elegance, this grave intensity of color, is cradled in your own slight heart. Even better, it's good to recognize that the beauty which speaks to you here is slumbering in the broken lives, the dim vision and bewildered stoicism of people to whom it has not been given to know what they have inside themselves.

Rain Storm

Rain.

Not much wind. Just enough to give a slight southern tilt to the rain. But water in such quantity you wonder the sky could hold so much. Rain in a hurry to get here. Not the gentle rainy-day-kind, but rain that can't wait, that doesn't care what happens to what it's coming down on.

People who didn't expect it come home in plastic or under boxes. I wish I had a picture of one barn worker zooming in on a bike, the top half of her in a plastic bag that billows out behind and sticks to her in front.

Sr. Kay is putting a cover on the garth fish pool so the goldfish won't float out and get beached.

Low retaining walls turn into frantic waterfalls. So do roofs. The lawns are now bayous. So urgent a rain mocks the earth's capacity for absorption. Water, once it gets here, has no place else to go.

This is nothing, I tell myself. I have seen monsoon pictures in *National Geographic*—a girl standing in her front yard up to her waist in water; a family watching TV with everyone's feet tucked up above the water level in the living room. Our rain is a trifle. Our rain is not a monsoon.

Still, you can't go away and forget it. It invades, annihilates, flattens, inundates your brain. Where are the chores you intended to get done in this piece of time? This piece of time has ceased to be a place to get things done in. It refuses to be useful. Either you take it on its own terms or you go away mad.

For the ancients, there was no such thing as an objective rain-storm. Nature was not objective, mechanical. It did not happen; it spoke. You did not study it; you listened to it.

I practice listening.

◊

In Common

The purpose of dialog is to send us away with something we didn't come with. Each of us brings a part of her experience, but the whole is greater than what anyone offers. We walk out with something no one brought all by herself, something created when experiences touch and words take light from one another.

My sisters have beautiful hearts. They are generous and understanding and they laugh at themselves, having learned to bend to the God of circumstance. Every day they teach me by being what they are. Today I learn from what they know.

We talk about conversion and work. Having recently interviewed an inquirer with eremitical preferences, I lap up my sisters' cheerful understanding of the common life. Some life-styles give you a lot of physical solitude in which to pray. Ours gives you silence in community. Silence is a climate of prayer, an interior solitude in the sharing of ourselves. You get the hang of it and feel sorry for people to whom this gift has not been given. Our individual prayer is intensified, orchestrated, magnified by the community prayer in which it finds its place.

Ask me what our life is, and before I have time to deal out subtleties, I will answer, "Community." Yes, it is God; yes it is prayer and transformation. But because God, prayer, and transformation come to us in Christ, our life is community. God is the common life, says Baldwin of Ford. And our common life is a sharing in his—a surrender to the gift of Father and Son to one another in the bond of the Spirit.

It's not my vocation to walk around in the kind of recollection that ignores another's need. My silence ought to glow with appreciation and encouragement. It's definitely wrong for me to fuss about the bad showing I will make if a fellow-worker sags at her end; or even about the extra time the job will take or the mess it's going to get into because somebody else isn't paying sufficient attention to holding up my image.

Thinking of work as a gift of oneself to the other takes a lot of pressure off. Naturally, you can't let someone act like a baby, still less give her the example of being one, and call it kindness. But you can offer her the demands of responsibility as compliments, acts of confidence in another's power to respond. The advantage to oneself comes in the yielding of the daily spotlight to another, the facing down of one's craving for advancement. You learn to enjoy the advancement of another in both competency and grace; in the ability to handle her strength and weaknesses lovingly. Someday you even get to enjoy being left behind.

Maybe Jesus is waiting for you there on some back road you are too anxious to get out of, some place where competency and status cease to barricade the heart, and the desire to give others the fullness they can only reach through your encouragement merges with the desire for God.

◊

Sulking

The world today is largely composed of mud and redwings. Its sky is china blue behind red maple blossoms. Maples waste no time in blossoming. The snow left only last week.

I didn't want to come out here. I much preferred to sulk, to nurse my losses and ignore the change of season. Having been so abusively treated by God, I wanted to show him that redwings weren't going to interest me this year. "If *you think* I'll play with your toys again after what you've done to me...."

But I've forgotten how awful I feel. And he says, "You only mourn because I'm not enough for you. How do you think I feel when you want so much other stuff more than you want me?"

Well, yes. Since you put it that way.

It's remarkable that the world has room enough for all its robins. Sometimes I feel it's overstocked with robins. But I am wandering from the conversation. You are speaking to me.

You say, "I am beautiful too. As beautiful surely as what you have not been given."

That's true. You've left me more than you took, and I want to explore it. Something is left and it's you.

◊

Dissonance

It's no one's destiny to be a wet blanket, and yes there is much more beauty and delight in our world than we want to give it credit for. It's our responsibility to take note of geraniums. But a lot of our good cheer has to grow out of the willingness to make friends with discordant circumstance, to cherish and receive it tenderly.

Our world must not be too congenial—our personal world, the place inhabited by our daily soul. There's more to life than the confirmation of personal preferences, and if we remain on the level of the soothing, we will miss out on what we are here for in the first place.

We should be turned back sometimes from our environment, from the surface of life where our instincts flash and play around the person we fancy ourselves to be.

We have to go deeper than reassurance. There's a place you wake up in one morning without quite knowing how you got there, a quiet which is not the romantic stilling of inner clamor but the loneliness of not being wrapped in the pleasant response of taste to taste, of taste to the object of its inclination. There's a whole country we have never mapped and don't know and are uneasy in. It's on the road. There isn't any detour. There's only going on or going back or sitting there.

Reality will never turn transparent to someone who clings to its appearances. Taste and the confirmation of oneself in sharing taste or opinions or outlooks, are introductory to life, not life itself.

"Trust me," says my circumstance. "This violation of your taste, this molding element, this fabric of small visitations: trust it. It is not an accident but an adventure, an advance, a deepening. Do you want to live in a mirrored hall or do you want to walk the hills and watch the sea?"

◇

The Tree

Accept the present.

Don't fuss because it does not fit your idea of prayer. God gives his idea of prayer. Let the wind blow your head clean. This self that climbs the hill, this unsatisfactory being, stuffed into a portable enclosure of about two cubic yards—let it park itself upon a bench and make peace with itself.

Let it not scratch at invisible walls as if God were outside and it could reach him only by being somewhere else, something else, someone else.

The pine branches heave like waves under a boat. This is a simple image, but don't try to be original as if originality of thought could rescue you from being who you are; as if the fresh and daring word could put you together in sight of some imagined looker-on. Lookers-on don't make you who you are.

The pine trunk doesn't move, but its branches do. I accept this symbol. Trees are holy images; they don't need to be dolled up with words. This image is the

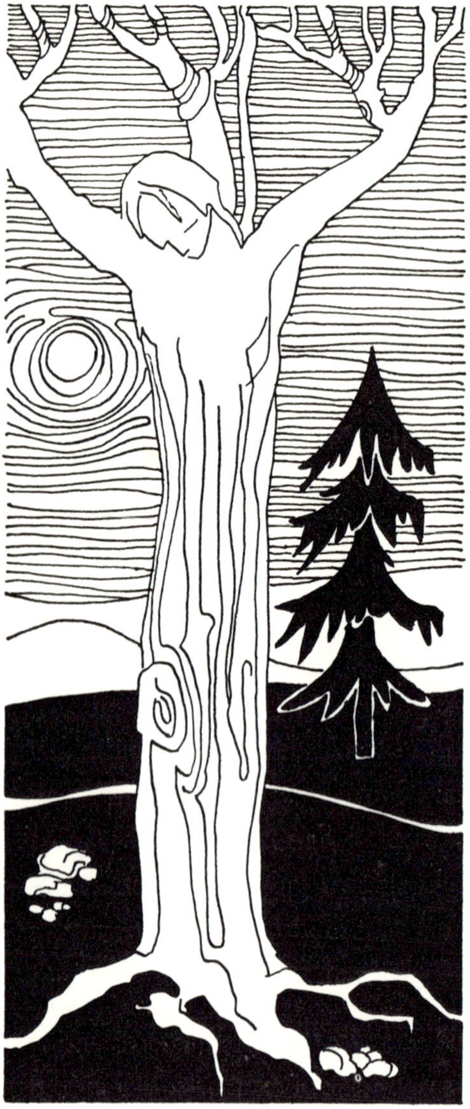

answer to my limited self, and the glory of it for that matter. I will not fight to be or to pray. I will sit up straight beside the tree and take what it gives me.

My roots go down, my trunk goes up, my branches move. God made trees in anticipation of hanging on one. He made them mean so much that his having been stuck up on one only brings out the meaning he had hidden in them from the beginning. God, as it were, came out of the tree, to teach what was hidden inside.

Come to terms with the meaning of the tree, be quiet with what is inside it. Its fingers press against the sky. Be simple, stop fussing. Let the new shoots grow.

◇

Easter

Hard to say a word about this morning except I did it all wrong and took personally every mechanical frustration. There was nothing to do but deal with the mess; every alternative was even less agreeable. Every alternative was impossible anyway, since I am no longer three years old and have learned that even a modified tantrum achieves nothing and loses a great deal of face.

The rest of the day is so cracked it won't hold anything. Somewhere on the other side of afternoon is night and sleep and next day and—ugh—remembering today.

Outside the Chapter Room window someone is starting a car we have borrowed while ours is indisposed. This one sounds as if it ought to be in the next bed. A deep-rose petunia turns into a blob of cotton candy through the frosted window glass.

Ah well.

I did badly but the cotton candy advises me that all is not lost. It embraces with good cheer asthmatic carburetors and the kind of people who make bad days for themselves and others.

One petunia in a window box, seen from this side of the glass, is a minor resurrection, a Passion symbol, an interpretation of innumerable bad days.

"They dressed him in a purple robe." Me too. Maybe it's pink. Anyway it's what my day looks like. Blood on a crown and cotton candy. Easter on a stick.

◊

Audience

That bird is a work of art, and there are so many of it, and they don't live long. How long does a purple finch live if the hawks don't get it? Such a brief being to be so finely made.

How long does a barn swallow live? Its flight is good theatre and I have a box seat. So much creative interest, so much tenderness went into its engineering. The world is full of entertainment. I feel it my duty to applaud the show.

◊

Now

I am not sitting here to get over the way I feel, to tinker and reorganize and put my parts back together in a more comfortable relation to each other. I'm here to agree to something, not to revise it; to put my hands around it and form them to its shape.

Even if the something is me.

Right now, right this minute, I am not being asked to make myself better, to plan my next disaster, to pacify my discontent. The raw skin over my self-esteem, the pulp of an assaulted identity are not at issue.

I put myself in my hands and hold it. I put my resentment of that self in my hands and form them around it. I lay in my lap the consequences of standing forth into a world that doesn't want me, can't make me who I want to be, has other interests and better things to do.

I forget about being quiet, and fold my disquietude in both my hands. What if I feel as if I were not worth the paper I'm written on? Is what I feel about myself so very important? I do not have to struggle through a thicket of disgust to find a place to pray in. My disgust is the place I currently have to pray in. I press my hands around my nothingness and curl them into its shape, laying my head against the knees of God. We are not going anywhere. Now is right here, and enough.

◊

The Bouquet

Daisies.

Thank you. They are my favorite flower and here they are. You have given us daisies, you hold out a bouquet. They have white petals and a golden yellow heart. The least I can do is notice, admire, and enjoy.

You might have made a world without daisies. There was no obligation. You didn't have to turn up at the door with this particular bunch of flowers. I'm glad you did. I'm going to put out my hands and accept.

All right, they are shastas, not real daisies. I saw them again this morning, a clump in the garth, crisp, starched, and contented with what they are expected to convey.

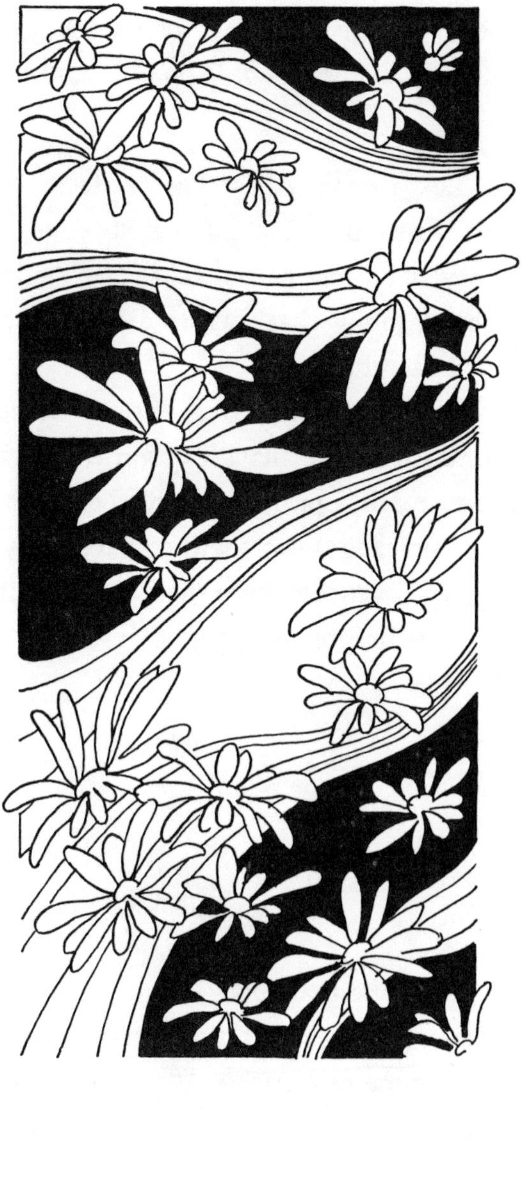

By noon, heat had melted out their starch. Their petals drooped. You feel sorry for soggy shastas dripping all over an afternoon. Who will send them rain?

Next day they have been watered, re-starched—and cut. Their days are numbered—one, two, maybe six. They stand in a pair of gold vases flanking the altar. It's nice to go out that way, to die in a state of worship, in such useful waste.

Cut flowers, however, unsettle me, even when they wind up on the altar. It's right of course. It's beautiful. They reach a peak of dignity before the end. I've seen the unpicked flowers wither before they fall. That too is sad. And yet they keep their contact with the earth, the sky, the irrepressible bugs.

◊

The Other

I can't be that good. I'm outclassed, outstripped, and over-arched. I wasn't made that interesting. I am neither champagne nor marble. What can I do with the people who are? Envy, weep, turn off the realization of being surpassed? Turn off half my switches and get on with my responsibilities?

There's not much future in that.

There has to be a better way to look at it, maybe this: Heaven will be God of course, unimaginable pleasure that will lie softly over our worn-out capacity for inferior enjoyment. But there will be more to it than that. We will delight in the place which everyone else has become.

Yes, place.

The beauty of each person will be something I can walk into—like woods or a vista seen from the hill. I will not feel dwarfed or diminished by the superior openness of other people for God, because their openness will be my pleasure. Their greater beauty will be for me like a park to which I am given access, a ballet for which I have an eternal box seat, the kind of book I would most love to sit with by a fire on a long winter evening.

And perhaps my greatest pleasure will be the deliverance from caring what happens to me. "Me" will be someone who can enjoy the other, take pleasure in the other's superiority, count the other's beauty as my own. "Me" will have become an exquisite joy at being the third jar from the left in the rear row on a shelf.

Loosening

God, trust is a gift.

I know as well as anyone and better than most how much a gift it is. I don't trust naturally. I worry.

Anxiety is an austere sin. Other sins have a litte fun attached, some pleasure, an advantage. Take adultery or fraud or pride. Anxiety is different. It only hurts.

Other sins *look* sinful too. You can't mistake them. But anxiety can look like a virtue. This makes it harder to kick. It is, however, more addictive than pleasure and quite definitely a vice.

Suppose I stop whatever I'm doing and look you in the face and say from the very bottom of my heart, "Please give me trust. Please make me a trustful person." And you say, "OK, but what will you give me in return?" And I know that you want only one thing; you want me to hand over my anxiety.

This is no small trade, you know.

You want my habit of anxiety, my addiction, my custom of looking carefully on every side for what is sure to go wrong, my cramped nerves and hard jaw— my determination to suffer ahead of time the thousand afflictions which might, and usually don't occur.

Maybe it's not worth the swap. I've got a lot to lose. I do a lot of defending that way. Nothing sneaks up on me. Nothing happens that I haven't counted on and got ready for and planned out in detail. What if you walked up and smashed me when I didn't have any skin on? Trust is for last ditches, when there's nothing else I could possibly do anyway.

And yet.

It occurs to me sometimes that my world might be waiting for me to loosen up. Maybe it can't come right until I do. Or maybe its being right is less important than the loosening process. Maybe, as a matter of fact, they amount to the same thing.

◊

How Not to Love

I could take my hands off, stop choking my world until its face turns blue. I could stop using anxiety as a way of getting back at you; curling up in a ball, rolling into a corner and spitting if you come too close.

What am I fighting anyway—objective circumstance or you?   I think I'd better start asking—regularly and systematically—for the gift of trust.

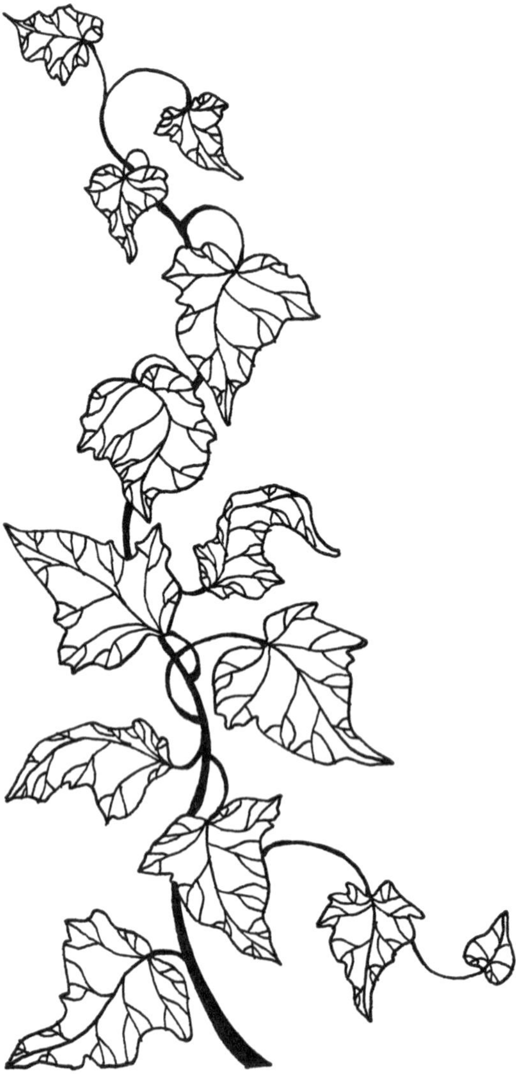

The Wound

There is no floor to the human heart. It has a hole in it so big it can't be filled with anything that begins and ends. It has a rent, a wound inside which no human hand or love can bandage, heal, or comfort.

You can give up something that exists, ratify the sacrifice of something you might have had. It's another thing entirely to accept the loss of what you never could have anyway because it does not exist—at least in the terms available this side of heaven.

You give your hurt to God and let him hold it. You stay there. Not on this earth will the emptiness be filled, the ache relieved. It gets buried, it hides. We think it has gone away. We're busy and satisfied with various enterprises.

Then something happens, or you read a book, see a film, bang your heart against a piece of beauty too good to be real life. The place inside which has no earthly correspondence is touched, and you go back to the God you thought you had domesticated.

"Later," you mumble to yourself, trying to impress him with your maturity, trying to tell yourself that nothing is wrong. "Later I will be filled. In eternity. Someday." It's a long wait. You can't tame the longing, you can't put a stopper in the discontent. "Later," you say, "I'm waiting." You agree to stop trying to manage a prayer that is only a want. Let him do it. You accept being an infinite incompletion with heartache around the edges.

And strangely, you are glad.

◊

Seeing

The Christmas crib.

You came to change things, Child. We forget, because nothing looks changed. Everything has the air of being what it has always been and always will be. Even the Christian churches usually seem about to cave in under the weight of human self-interest.

You came to improve our condition, and your having been denied and crucified and raised from the dead shouldn't have voided your intention. We should be improved. You must have done what you came for. What's the matter? In particular, what's the matter with me?

It might be me of course. I am the matter with me. Nothing can be done in someone who refuses to let it be done. Nothing can be seen by someone who refuses to see. Nothing can be given to someone who refuses the gift.

When things are not so bad, I am relieved. When they are not so good, I summon up my stock of Christian fortitude. "Don't expect much," I always say.

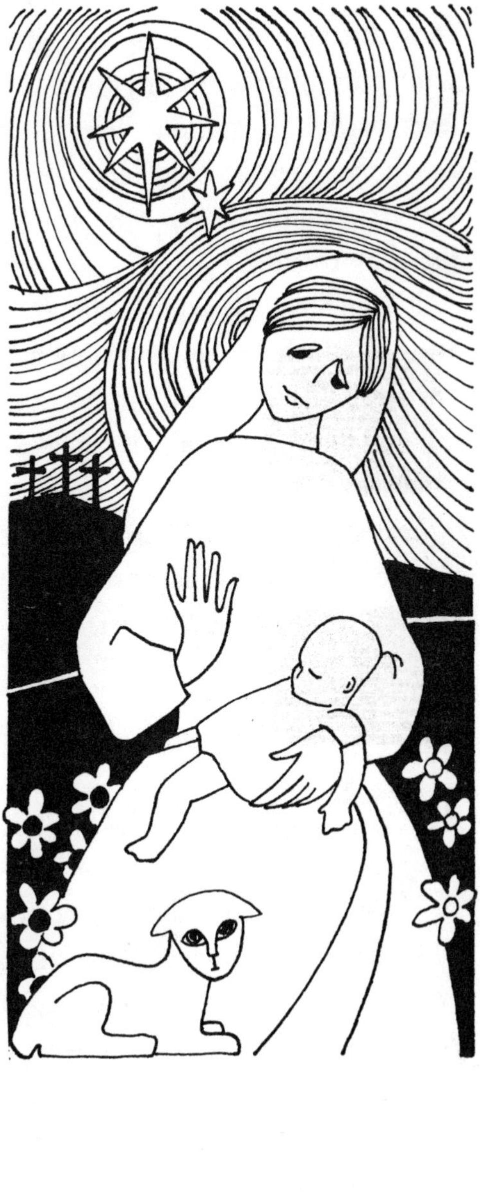

The heck with Christian fortitude, with bearing contradiction and putting up with fatigue. The heck with putting up with anything. There are people who lead hard and glorious lives, and they never bear anything. They are too busy loving, too busy mining every circumstance for its store of gemstone. They are too busy trusting.

It's often not the exterior circumstance but the interior attitude which creates the happy person. This is a cliche. I'm sorry. It would be a pity to miss out on life because the way to use it properly is being expressed in unoriginal language.

Expect much. Don't narrow your expectations because you are afraid of being hurt. See much, see more than you are willing to see, deeper than you feel you can.

◊

Today

Today won't come back tomorrow.

Often joy gets buried in the struggle to be rid of what we don't like about today, or to get done what we want so desperately to get done. (There's a difference between doing things and doing things to get them finished.) Joy, we feel, should be unadulterated by what is wrong with today, and so we put it off until we get more favorable conditions.

So much is here to be loved. And yet usually, "This is wrong and that is unbearable and if I don't resolve this difficulty immediately, it will chew up my brain." Plod, plod.

What if all we had were today? Would we want to leave the last day of our earthly life unexplored, unappreciated, and unloved? For some of us, life never seems to fit right. We're never here, even though we're technically alive. This has to be wrong.

Today, this hour, this moment wrap in their commonalities, burdens, and contradictions, the sweet surprises of God. We must develop a skill for unwrapping inelegant parcels if we want what is hidden inside.

Today is a secret whispered in a noisy room. We have to learn how to hear.

This minute is a husk around a joy that will remain untasted if we don't cultivate the ability to peel.

◊

Bloodstream

What's the matter?

Everything's the matter. Look at the world you made. Look around. It hurts to think about, and there's nothing I can do.

Pray for it. Why don't you pray?

That's a good question. I should be honest: I have a number of worries, discontents, and disturbances all my own. Being magnetic, they limit my concentration on other things. They are not really objective reactions to circumstance but chronic symptoms of a sense of inadequacy. Therefore they have no solution and only gum up the works.

Secondly, the world doesn't show much inclination to get better. It's as if: so I pray for it, so it spits in my eye. I feel like a moth in a steel mill. Such is my effect upon your world. I've never been good at "praying for the world." I want to give my life for the world, help it by absorbing it into my own conversion. That sounds noble. I try, but I get so tired.

"Praying for the world" sounds inadequate. I realize this is a psychological aberration, and that I haven't got an accurate idea of what is involved. Well maybe. And maybe what I haven't got is faith.

Prayer for the world isn't measured by my limitations. Praying for the world is like slipping into its bloodstream and knowing that the blood is Christ's. It's letting go and believing that these moments of presence to its hurts and disabilities, to its beauty and accomplishments, are healing moments. They give life because he does, and his prayer is what I'm bringing into bruised and infected places.

Prayer for the world means not letting your vision be

cramped by what you determine is there to be seen. Prayer for the world means hope. I remember a vocational inquirer who told me that our monastery wasn't nearly far enough out in the country. "Look at the ugly red glare in the sky at night."

Well, there *is* a glow above the hills to the south. I have never thought it ugly. It's gentle like sunrise, and when the clouds are particularly placed, it can be beautiful. I always admire it out the kitchen window when locking up on winter evenings. Way over there, out of sight or hearing, lies the city of Providence. It has its deficiencies, but I think Roger Williams' city is aptly named. It gives a sunrise to the night sky. We have to believe in sunrises.

Or to put it negatively, we have to let go of our refusal to believe in what we cannot see. Prayer is an act of confidence, a cutting free from our anger at a world which does not re-style itself to our satisfaction.

This great thing I can do, this is my privilege and my joy. I lean into the prayer of Christ, into his offering. I run into it after the fashion of young children into the sea. It carries me. It carries the world.

Come In

Everything beautiful between people is sacramental, imaging a reality beyond itself. It does more than image; it partakes of what it symbolizes, but that is not my point right now.

Think of the most perfect and abiding human friendship or the loveliest experience of romantic love, the deepest relationship founded in affinity and the transcendence of affinity. Consider the most triumphant journey through the difficulties of married or parental love. You have then an image of prayer.

Prayer is determining to accept our situation. It's deciding to be where we are; and where we are is in the Spirit of God. The Spirit is not only our home. The Spirit is the meeting place of two loves—the Father and the Son—so absolute and simple that they are one. It's nice to be invited in, especially when the place is not really a place but the exchange itself, and is so personal that it is also a person.

We say of two human lovers that "they shared a great love," as if the love were something in itself. This expression bears a likeness to the reality we are given in prayer. For the Spirit is that—a great love.

You go crazy trying to equalize the Trinity in words without ironing all the interest out of it. The Spirit is a great love. I'd like to say it that way and maintain my orthodoxy.

All those denials—"My children, how hard it is for a rich man...." All those denials are only to keep the images from crowding out the reality—or, more properly, to keep us from mis-using the symbol in such a way that it shrinks our capacity for the real.

"Remain in my love." Stay. Sit, root, be, come in out of the night. Be walled by the Spirit, who is the place in which all human loves, all human beauties, come home to find what it is they are reflecting. Nothing complicated is being asked. But the human heart can find it very taxing to be simple.

◊

The Road

We can't always relax in order to pray. We try, but find by the end of the session that we haven't done yet what we intended to do and thought we already had done at the beginning. Nothing went wrong, nothing that is, except God. He has a way of leading us around in circles. He takes over our prayer in order, among other things, to show us a tension we didn't know we had.

It's customary to think we can let go all by ourselves, with a good method and a little help from grace. But praying is meeting someone who knows better and has other ideas of where we should be headed. He takes us there even though we don't know the way or have any intention of winding up in such a strange place.

We have to be careful, on this and other occasions, not to throw away the prayer because it doesn't suit us or conform to our expectations.

Some prayer is messy because we just don't care enough—or know how—to keep it in order. We let it ooze out through every crack in our heads, resentful that we have to pray when we'd rather be doing something else, determined to solve a problem right now, a problem God is not going to *let* us solve until we've made an effort to take our hands off.

But some prayer is confused by God's design, even by God's nature. We become confused because we are being led and don't recognize the road. He will not permit us to get on as we intended. Or we are confused because the someone we have met is not the someone we expected him to be.

Now and then it can seem that he is not leading, but standing in our way. Every possible path is blocked, every road to everywhere. And the most uncomfortable thing about it is that this kind of prayer can seem to be a dry run for the rest of life—"Lord, there's no place to *go!*"

There is. He'll go back to leading, once we've made our peace with being blocked.

Rock Formation

"Good master, what should I do to inherit eternal life? What is still lacking to me?"

Oddly, this gospel passage says a lot about praying for the world. I wonder what this fella thought when he heard about Jesus' death? That he'd had a close call and wasn't he lucky to have got away free?

Free. Good master, what is lacking to me?

How free am I? How flexible? Just praying for the world isn't enough. Or rather, I can't share deeply enough in Jesus' prayer for others unless I am free to give myself to it. And I'm not free if the weight of self-concern has pressed my inner world into a hunk of rock that can't be dissolved, chipped, carved, or eroded.

What is lacking? Or maybe, what shouldn't be there?

Worry. Calculation. Self-protection, manipulation, pose, terror, apprehension, anxiety.

We can pray for the world with part of ourselves and hold on to its values with what is left. "Lord, I am not like the rest of men. I even pray for them."

Dear child, you cannot pray for the world until you recognize the world in your own heart. Hold up to me, not somebody else's sin but your own, not somebody else's want of faith but yours. Only when you can see somebody else's want in your own attitudes can you help to heal the other. It's your own rock formation that has to be given over to the elemental forces of my freeing love.

Let go. Let go of this constant anxiety about the impression you make, about yesterday's slip and tomorrow's blunder and how and where to apply the makeup. This dither over why another person's life isn't going as you feel it should. This fever to have it your way. I can run things but no one would ever know it by a look at what's inside you. Give me your concern, your tension, your compulsive attachment to the fixing-up of things, so I can crack it from within. Then maybe you'll see what I can do for the world.

What are you lacking? Child, you know quite well.

◊

Grief

Grief is the heart's response to loss. Grief is totality, even in its milder forms, because we are physical beings. There is no such thing as purely spiritual grief, because there is no such thing as a purely spiritual human being. We meet and deal with life in a complexity of body and spirit which becomes more baffling the more we know about it.

Our simplest, even our most peripheral wants are enmeshed in blood, nerves, glands, brain, muscles. Emotions run in the bloodstream. Loss is not an immaterial occurrence. It invades the cells.

Grief is the response to losing a person, a place, a

position, a form of labor, a capability. It is the reaction to an experience of want or diminishment, the cry after some emotional satisfaction given by something which has become part or even most of our personal being, and now is gone. It can even be a reaction to the loss of a satisfaction we have never actually experienced except in desire or expectation.

Grief has affinities to disease. According to its nature and intensity, it can feel like cancer, flu, or hives, and it is not much more controllable. We know all the answers; we wish we did not feel the way we do, think the way we do. We want our bodies to work properly and our minds to function as if they really coincided with the convictions we know we have.

And yet there is this thing, this dull grey blanket thrown over our heads, this succession of thoughts we hate ourselves for thinking. We grow tired of fighting these angry, self-pitying, petty, jealous, hating thoughts. We know they are not thoughts at all, but emotions that have moved in to operate the mental apparatus without anybody's permission. The primal instincts have been assaulted, and we feel around desperately for the button that will turn them off. Our real thoughts, our permanent convictions, seem to be crushed in the gears. Here is the pain, so wrenching or suffocating or paralyzing that to drag oneself from morning to night is only slightly less awful than thrashing from the beginning to the end of night.

Recipe

Grief has several advantages which we appreciate best from the perspective of having got out of it. We tend to think best when not being mashed.

One of these advantages is the experience of God's resistance to being used. He is not a switch that you throw to further your plans for virtue, success, or the establishment of a better self-image.

We should certainly try to approach life with the proper attitude. But we can easily develop a wrong attitude toward the cultivation of a proper attitude, and grief does us the favor of showing us this. To scout out, instead of trampling, the small joys of life; to see a glorious gift in undistinguished wrapping paper; to learn the art of interpreting the languages of God's love—all this is an exigency of faith.

But we can, in the process of pursuing Christian joy, entertain a few questionable assumptions; and the most destructive is the one which expects God to provide what we're demanding if we fulfill a number of specified requirements.

Joy, we think, is the outcome of responding to the circumstances of life in an attitude of faith. Therefore, if this attitude is correctly applied to each circumstance, God is obliged to come through with our allotted portion of Christian joy. We have the recipe for a better self—a joyful Christian with whom God has to be pleased. "I thank you Lord, that I am not like other people—sad sacks, depressed and pessimistic."

We would rather trust a system than trust God. We would rather pull a lever than look into the eyes of Christ. Sometimes I think we would prefer a machine in good working order to a friend—when the friend is God.

This inclination is what God is uncovering when we are slapped by some failure, when our emotional house gets flooded. We find that faith is not a matter of the proper cookbook. Sometimes it is a matter of climbing onto the kitchen table till the flood waters recede.

Our attempts at virtue are not wrong, our willingness to see right. Our conviction that joy grows out of faith is not wrong either. Our trouble lies in the how of it.

A friendship is not a machine, and grace is not an ingredient in a recipe. Love is not a form into which we pour the concrete of our determination to be deserving of approval.

Grief is no fun at all, but at least it teaches us a little more about how to be a friend.

The Path

Every day, in every weather, I get a walk through the woods. It comes with my job, because the woods lie between the place I start from and the place I work in. (Sunday walks are optional, but I often take the same route to the hayfield.) "Woods" is rather a grand title, but "copse" sounds British and affected; and though my little stand of maples, pine, fern, moss, rocks and other things is quite inconsequential, I might as well call it a woods and be done with it.

The path runs north and south, beginning with a hole in the forsythia hedge, and ending between the tool shed and the blueberry patch. Ahead is sky and, in season, vegetables. This year the land is bearing string beans and cauliflower.

This direction is not without significance. If a path runs through a piece of woodland north and south, and you are heading north, the low morning sun lights from behind all the leaves at your right hand. The world is more exciting when its sun comes at you through the leaves.

This principle applies in winter also, even without snow. Light that curls around the birch trunks from behind creates a far more interesting place than light that falls over your shoulder to erase the third dimension of the approaching landscape. Light that meets you on your way actualizes the potential glory of an ordinary prospect.

And then of course there's snow. Snow is at its best when sun is meeting you head-on across a snowy path, or when, coming from the side, it throws long shadows at your feet. Shadows, as the Impressionists well knew, are not grey. Snow shadows especially are not grey. Each day, each time of day, determines its own palette. Snow is not white either, but anything at all depending on its mood. Some days it glitters like a rainbow.

Sun is not the only master of my woods.

Rainy mornings, mornings after rain, sulky mornings, and undecided ones—every day I get some kind of show. Who knows what I owe to this little path that takes me every morning to the north.

◊

Running

I wish the air would dry; I feel like a flounder. But I can be so anxious for release from a sub-tropical climate that I have no eye for the gentleness of fog.

I am too anxious in general to get on to something else; my very manner of walking betrays that I am never home. I am an exile but not a pilgrim. I have become my restlessness, for I am never here, always heading toward the next thing to be done.

A state of exile from oneself is not good. There's exile

and exile, and some of it is constructive, but not this. I must go home.

"Come to me, all who labor, and I will give you rest." Am I running *from* something or *toward* something? What is there to run to? The great satisfaction of getting things done?

"Come to me." Where? Well, not out there, not where I'm running to. Running is not the definition of human life. Neither is checking things off on a list.

"Come."

I have to enter my heart, my circumstance, my present. I have to come home.

◊

Deep

I read about a lake so deep its surface turns a special shade of blue. The point is obvious. I've also read of an oriental prayer method in which you imagine yourself a pebble sinking slowly to the bottom of a pond. (I find it helpful to envisage a sleepy summer pond far distant from human complications, attended by the hums and squeaks, the dragon-flies and frogs of some still afternoon.)

The point is that there's someplace else to go, there's something to sink into. We don't have to live forever on the surface, rocked by our emotional reactions to every trifle—or even every genuine responsibility—that ruffles the upper waters of concern.

I won't find answers on the surface. I won't even find the right questions. A certain constancy attends the exploration of the lake bed, a certain confidence in this form of education. It simplifies. It waits.

◇

What's Wrong

What about those days when something seems to be wrong, but we can't put a finger on it? God is out to lunch or taking a nap or concerned with a project in which we have no place. God is a lump of dough on a cold radiator. All the explanations fit somebody else's problem, but not ours. The problem itself is not the problem, but not knowing what's wrong.

What have I done which I should be undoing? My gaze sticks to myself like a barnacle to a rock. God, let me find an explanation, a method.

Why not shift the gaze? Why? How? My eyes smart with fog. What is there to see?

Trust is a form of vision. It sees the fog or the unbroken stretch of tundra not as sterile and repellant but as personal, mysterious, and beckoning.

We don't have to understand. That may be the whole point of the situation. We may be asked simply to agree to the suspension of our desire to understand.

At this moment, Lord, give me trust. Show me if I am doing something wrong, if by my fault your presence has evaporated. Show me what to do if you want something done. But if this obstruction mediates your presence, then give me patience with it, reverence for it. Help me love it, and give me joy in it, the plain joy of trusting that instead of separating us, this sense of your absence draws me into your arms.

◊

Gladness

Lord, are you satisfied with me? Right now, here, this moment? Am I all right, or would you prefer me to be otherwise, to be doing something else? I look into your face. No, it's all right. You're not asking for this moment anything except my being here beside the potato patch trying to pray.

Swallows don't sing. They don't need to. Their flight takes care of everything. They can afford to squeak. The world is currently full of swallows. It's as if they were telling me how much you care that I am trying to trust in your love for me.

I could not have more than I have right now; nothing I could gain would enrich me further. When what you have is infinite, there's no place else to go. Just being rich, being loved is a prayer. Just not cringing, just being grateful and glad.

◇

Tomorrows

I dread next Saturday. If it could only come and be over. Going through it would be less difficult than looking at it from two days ahead.

I suppose I could use a little faith.

Faith is not merely a respectful nod to a list of propositions. It is recognizing the truth behind those propositions when it turns up at work, in a personal relationship, in change or loss or humiliation, in weariness or confusion, as well as in the common joys we tend to take for granted. Faith is the currency of the present, good for today, for this hour, this moment.

If I run ahead, trying to live in my personal projection of the future, I outstrip the now without any faith in my pocket. I am a vagrant in a world which does not yet exist and will never exist as I imagine it. I will not be given the faith with which to deal with tomorrow until it gets here, and never at all if it doesn't.

Faith can handle difficulty. It can deal somehow or other with grief, great or small, take a dustcloth to unappreciated joys. But only if I do not dictate the manner in which it should. Faith is not an abstraction; it is the acceptance of a person, the acknowledgement that circumstance is not a thing but someone, someone I know quite well.

◊

Blue

Blue is not my favorite color, but what can you do when there's so much sky? You like blue anyway, especially the kind of clean fall sky that carries a large supply of lighted clouds. You learn to like what you do not have a natural affinity for. You grow and you grow richer.

Like this morning. The sun came up. Nothing spectacular happened, no splashy sunrise. At first the sky was just a little lighter than the trees. Then it turned grey, then lumpy like a pudding not quite mixed, then mother-of-pearl. This took some time. I kept waiting for something to happen, but nothing did. Behind my back a few patches of blue fell free of clouds. That's all. The sky came back and it was blue. I will not argue with God.

Lakes are blue and so is the ocean which I love. I used to wonder why the sea was blue at a distance and green close-up (and colorless for that matter in your hands). I know there's an answer and that it is less interesting than the question. A lot of life is like that. A lot of life is just a matter of learning to like blue.

◊

Letter to a Friend

My little friend, your life is all knotted into mystery. You finger the threads but the knots stay put, and leave you holding several problems you want solved. You don't know what the solutions are going to ask of you, or what they are going to look like, or whether when they turn up you will recognize them as solutions at all.

I don't know either. I would like to fix things my way. I tug at the knots and the knots grow tighter as if to warn me off. All I learn is that I can't force knots. God does not yield to force.

He does not yield to rush or to our determination to get things settled. He has use for seasons of uncertainty. He also has use for moments of decision, and some knots ask simply for a knife. It's sometimes easy and sometimes hard to know what kind of knot you're dealing with.

I take the threads in both my hands, carrying them to the God of patience and careful Providence. Part of the process is knowing what I can't yet do and may never be able to do. Part of it is keeping watch beside the hands which in their own time will attend to snarls, kinks, knots, and ill-chosen colors.

◇

Recovering

Someone tells me he has trouble accepting himself as an alcoholic. He has three years of sobriety with AA. I remember a story told us by a great spiritual master:

Professional obligations had forced him into a cocktail party where he felt bored and alien. Then he met someone whose personality quietly set a light in his dreary afternoon. This man was a psychiatrist, unpretentious, witty, warmly enthusiastic and interested in other people. His presence was in itself a kind of redemption.

Asking around, our friend found out that his new acquaintance was a member of AA. He had lost his family, his profession, friends, money and self-respect. He had, in fact, spent several years on the street. Now he was back, but more than back. He had done more than recover a lost life. He had found a life richer and deeper than the one he had lost. He was more now to himself, God, and the world he was ministering to than if he had never had a problem with alcohol.

To accept oneself as an alcoholic, to accept the profound spirituality of AA, is to accept oneself as a favored child of God, a special channel of grace. I know two brothers, one of whom is the other's AA sponsor. But in a deeper sense, the AA member has a special bond of kinship with Christ in all his wounded and needy members, and that means every one of us.

◊

Yellow

I like yellow.

Not by itself of course, and not every shade. Not yellow as in lemons, not the kind that turns into chartreuse behind your back. But yellow as in buttercups, as in the center of a daisy—yellow with warmth.

Yellow is not independent like green or even like blue. Green or blue get along by themselves. A green world is pleasant. It would be agreeable even without petunias. A blue sky can reach from one horizon to another without oppressing you. But a yellow sky for more than a sunset would make you nervous. Yellow trees are fanciful. You wouldn't want twelve months of autumn.

Yellow depends.

It looks well with other colors—ivory, green or brown. Think of dandelions in the hay, buttercups along the road. Rust and burnt-orange embrace it. It needs. It must have something other than itself. I am fond of sunlight in jars of marmalade, (and wonder if Anne Lindbergh has carried this taste into old age). There is yellow in the haze of morning trees. Yellow relates, emphasizes, collaborates, and gets along with. Perhaps this has something to do with its function as an expression of happiness.

◊

The Shining Cloud

Four hawks.

But hawks don't usually approach too closely. They don't appreciate the carrot patch where I am sitting. I would like to do a few more meditations, but I can't. I think I can no longer do this sort of thing.

It's amazing how quickly the carrots have picked up since they were thinned and weeded. On weeding day the situation was yard-high weeds and two-inch carrots. Maybe I am being weeded. That's quite all right. It's interesting, and who needs more meditations.

I would say the same thing over:

We are not joyful because the world is uniformly good or pleasant or beautiful but because it is redeemed, because it carries in its heart a resolution that our tenderness and faith can warm and bring to life.

We have to spend time at the quiet job of finding, holding, giving warmth to the seeds of redemption—in all that is cramped and dislocated, in all that is graceful and harmonious. It's very simple. We must burrow down to a place beneath the complexity we manufacture for ourselves, spend some time there being still—not fussing, not writing meditations.

The hayfield is being mowed, and swallows, evicted from the near-by trees, protest the tractor with their acrobatics.

What do you know? Two hawks. Three. Hawks very close—with a bit of interest in the carrots? Hawks are predators but their flight is lyrical. The problem of hawks will be resolved in heaven. I have half an idea of how, but I don't know for sure.

The swallows, meanwhile, have prudently beat it. One never knows with hawks. So I will end where I began, with swallows and hawks, but not with fog. Today has a proper kind of sky—bright blue with fat white clouds. God has predilection for the shining cloud.

A YEAR LATER

July Fourth

Half-holiday.

It's only nine o'clock and already we have had adventures. From breakfast til Chapter time, Mother, Sr. Luanne, Brother, and then Greg labored to unlock, to unhinge, and finally to hack through a door in the guesthouse. It had stuck shut on one of the retreatants. I'm sure everyone including the captive had a great time—better than a flood even. But the door is a wreck. We will have to get a new one.

After Mass, the Fourth of July Orchestra (two guitars, one flute, one recorder, and a set of drums) accompanied the national anthem. My only complaint about this annual event is that we only get to sing one verse. You just get steamed up and have to quit. It ends, however, with an impressive retard and a lot of stuff on the drums—which compensates.

Patriotic songs choke me up, especially on the high notes. And the drums make me laugh. So I am not much help with the singing. Our congregation is now used to July-Fourth-at-the-Monastery and takes us for granted. Our first rendition, several years ago, took them by surprise and they burst into applause. We were embarrassed but it's nice to be appreciated.

Now I am outside, trying to forget that I have five half-hour classes to plan for the novices while Sr. Maureen is at a meeting. My initial horror at the prospect was a black and unrelenting moment: "I don't *know* anything!"

We will get along. They will do the work and I will organize. At least I will if my head unsticks. Maybe I need a hatchet too.

◊

Lightly

Trust.

People you've given away come back or they will come back in heaven, or they have, on some deep level, never left. Beauty you've lost turns up again more beautiful than ever. You don't really need to solve the problems you've been chewing for a day, a month, a year.

I have so much to worry about I get mental indigestion at the prospect of making a list. I'm afraid of forgetting something I should dedicate a few tense muscles to. My responsibilities are my self, my name, my slot in a board marked *value*. This cannot go on.

Trust is knowing that the clock will go around more efficiently if I don't hang on its hands. The world will get disentangled from itself if I am less hell-bent on picking its knots. My responsibilities will get somewhere interesting if I can set sail lightly into an adventure whose unexpected and exotic landfalls are too easily unnoticed by the sailor whose hand lies heavy on the wheel.

◊

Rejoicing

My soul glorifies the Lord.
My spirit rejoices in God my savior.
It can afford to. That's what we are made for. That's what we're on earth for, companions of trees and springs and blueberry bushes—even if the trees are only the kind that struggle out of steel fences in a world of concrete.

We came to rejoice in God our savior, to know what it means to be saved, to want to be saved from petty self-display, from a preference for redecorating the universe according to our own taste, from deeper and more radical forms of not being able to receive.

There's so much in the world that's terrible. Can I really walk into the sub-cellars of my heart and rejoice that an adaptable Paradise is cracking its way through the floor, velveting its walls, rioting in scented darkness? It's not precisely the Paradise I would have planned. There are times when I take a dim view of the landscape artist. But he deserves a little appreciation.

My faith in what he can do—here in me—will

become an invisible power, making others available to his services. Faith works that way. I must have faith in what he can and will do in them. Then we can all grow grass in the right places. But this will not happen if all I contribute to their reclamation project is the sulks—on their or my account.

◊

Looking The Other Way

"The world is so full of a number of things."

Indeed. But they do not all make us happy as kings. The world is full of beauty, but also of evil and of disagreeable situations. Some of these we must notice and work to improve. That's obvious. But we have an equally firm responsibility to ignore many others. It's important to know the difference.

The irritating quality of someone's personality is often one of the things I am better off not meditating on; or the dusty corner in which I seem to have been parked; or the array of concerns labelled, "Someone else's business." Minding one's own business is still a virtue in a culture which feels there is no such thing as someone else's business.

Noticing and knowing too much will shrink instead of broadening me. My emotional reactions to a multitude of stimulations, especially exasperating ones, can lock me into a mental prison more unrelenting and degrading than a civil correctional institution. Not only has someone locked me in; someone has entered my mind and sat down at the controls, printing out all manner of painful propaganda. I am possessed by the people who threaten or irritate me, or more properly, by my reactions to their aberrations, their real superiorities, or their better luck.

The look on someone's face, an opinion I don't agree with, a violation of my taste can walk right inside and determine whether I'm going to be happy or miserable today. I have delivered up my world—not to another person exactly, but to my reactions to another person. I have given myself away to a species of torture I could escape if I a) didn't look, and b) thought about something other and better.

For simply ignoring is not enough; absorption in something else is the second step. If I were at a concert, the music would pour in, pressing so firmly against my inner walls that it wouldn't leave room for jealousy, carping, irritation, or greed. I would give my heart to the richness of the music.

A concert is not always handy, and anyway music is only a modest finite expression of the God I always have. I have so great a love to stretch to. Christ is my music, my horizon, my sea, and my green woods. Paradox: by disciplining my attention, I see farther, dig deeper, receive more abundantly.

Is this what I want? The bright peace of Christ within? Is it enough for me? To how many things have I given the power to bother me. How angry, sad, uneasy, and unpleasant have I become over trivialities whose outcome I have not remembered a few weeks later. If my discontent had wished them away, or had they never existed, I would not have been at peace. For a peace that depends on the vagaries of circumstance is much too fragile to hang onto.

A peace that lasts must depend on what's inside—a preference for the peace of Christ, and a willingness to turn from the aggravations that unsettle it.

◊

The Well

"It is absurd to look for a well, at random, in the immensity of the desert." So said St. Exupery in *The Little Prince*, before discovering that such a quest was not as crazy as he'd thought.

What about me?

For instance: Some people are difficult to live with. They hurt others because they are hurt themselves or because they have not been given agreeable personalities. Sometimes a pair of big feet wander in to squash the seedlings with which I have tried to decorate my personal wilderness. Is it then so absurd to look for a well, at random, in the immensity of the desert? Whose desert? Mine and someone else's. A co-operative wilderness.

Maybe it is absurd, "but nevertheless, we started walking." What is compassion? Is it thinking gently of someone whose suffering you feel good about sharing? Is it anger at whoever has made a mess of another's life? Maybe it's both and something else beside, something you only discover on that hike through the dry wash of shared human deprivation.

Maybe compassion is the acceptance of pain wrought in me by another's anger or fear or sense of inadequacy; the willingness to bear another's loneliness by bearing its effect on me, its assault upon my need to be appreciated, competent, lovable.

It's easier to love a difficult person if you love yourself. And perhaps the well in the desert is at least partially that—the courage to love yourself, the faith to accept your worth from the most secure of all possible sources, and to agree to this self and this value, a value which can never fall to any exterior assault.

"And as I walked on so, I found the well, at daybreak."

St. Exupery said "I", because he was carrying his friend.

Christ of the desert well, make me content with the simple springs of what I am, so happy with what you've made me that how I feel about myself can never force me to resent another person. Show me how to find in me and in every companion of my desert wandering the water that can feed a green and fragrant landscape, an inner world of pasturage and rest.

"What makes a desert beautiful is that somewhere it hides a well."

◇

Wine

There is, of course, another side to it. I too am a wrecker of gardens. Or at least one who fails to cultivate the other's wilderness and plant daffodils among the rocks. I too get on other people's nerves; I think more about what's wrong with my world than what I can do to improve someone else's. Other people have to accompany *me* to the spring.

I'm grateful that they do, but I have to say that this kind of gratitude does not come easily. Lord of desert places and of hidden springs—water if you please this dry bush which is me. You understand how hard it is to accept forgiveness, to entrust to the understanding of other people a personality desiccated by self-interest and stunted from want of generosity.

What have I learned in these two weeks? Principally, I think, that we must give what we have and be what we are. What I am is this fiercely limited being who has to try to love. And love usually means giving one's limitations to the other. Limitation is the place where a real good comes to an end. We must not withhold the good because we're discontented with the extent of its perimeter. Laying your discontent on the line is part of the good you have to give.

Help me to see that what I am (and am not) is not all there is to me, not all I have to give. Whether what we are giving is part of a monastic or of a lay Christian tradition, the tradition is Christ—Christ exercising the art of freeing his people for love, the art of dying and the art of breaking into tulips and forsythia when we feel the calendar has got stuck in February. The power of Christ is not impeded by my deficiencies. Maybe he gets a kick out of coming across in spite of (and sometimes because of) my deficiencies.

Plant me in the humus of your mortal heart, Jesus-gardener, and let me draw from it the sap of immortal wine. I and my patient friends would enjoy a banquet now and then. They deserve it; I'm not sure about me, but I'd appreciate it too.

Consider

But even this is far from everything. It is the smallest part of everything. If our lives are enriched by the willingness to find a poignant beauty in all that is limited and deficient in ourselves and others, we are equally gifted by all that is right in ourselves and others; and in the particular beauty created by the interrelation of deficiency and strength.

Consider the wonder of an older person, someone whose roots have found nourishment in the truth of Christ; someone whose quiet encounter with common trial and common joy has stacked her life's barn with a rich and surprising harvest—trust, humor, the wry acceptance of loss and gift, a unique response to the unexpected approaches of a God whose major policy seems to be throwing your expectations off-balance.

Count—or try, and fail to count—how constant and varied is the support of others: here is someone whose journey into God is written down for you in a smile, an ability to understand; here is someone who has penetrated a world of values which makes light of all the troubles you bring upon yourself by clinging to a set of trivial compensations for losses you are meant to accept and move on from.

Or watch the young, taking their first steps into a country whose map they cannot read and whose roads are not renowned for street lights and highway improvements.

How much we receive from the conversion of their first enthusiasm into a solid willingness to keep on going, to gain a taste for new and subdued forms of revelation, for occasional vistas and frequent blisters on the heel. How much we gain from their newness, from a share in the way they see—freshly and from unexpected angles—a process we have grown used to: the surrender of one's deepest heart into the adventure of God.

◊

Doors

God has a way of opening doors I don't want to go through. I know the room I'm in, the house and its furniture and the tiling on the floor. I could put a hand against the spot on the wall touched by the sun at four o'clock on a December afternoon. Somebody please shut the *door*.

I remember one of these invitations. Outwardly, the trial was insignificant: an instance of not getting my own way. Inwardly, it was one of the most emotionally complicated situations of my life.

I had no choice about doing what was asked; that is often the way with our most difficult decisions. My only real freedom lay in the choice of *how* I was to do what must be done.

This is a door, I said to myself. The how of this situation is a way of stepping through. On the other side is growth and grace and going on. On this side is unhappiness and the betrayal of myself and God. So I didn't pout. But this was no great virtue. I knew that if I didn't pass through this time, the door would open again in some other form. I would have to go through someday, somehow—unless God were to give me up to counting the progress of December sun across a wall, and leave me to my own betrayal.

He held his own end up, I must say. The road that led away from the far side of the door was shadowed and rocky but it got somewhere. I walked into some of the best graces of my life, graces that in the following year, I could never have done without.

Now I like to think of doors, gates, or even stiles. They aren't always as momentous and obvious as that one, but they always lead somewhere. They can be so ordinary that I am tempted to complain about my current annoyance just *because* it's so inconsequential—a little more dignity, please. But if I see it as a doorway, it beckons with unquestionable importance. It promises, it reassures. No circumstance is too insignificant to raise a lintel over my head and invite me to a further stage of the journey.

Let me not throw away my chances. Let me not pass by these little doors because they are too modest to be taken notice of. The door may creak on hinges as simple

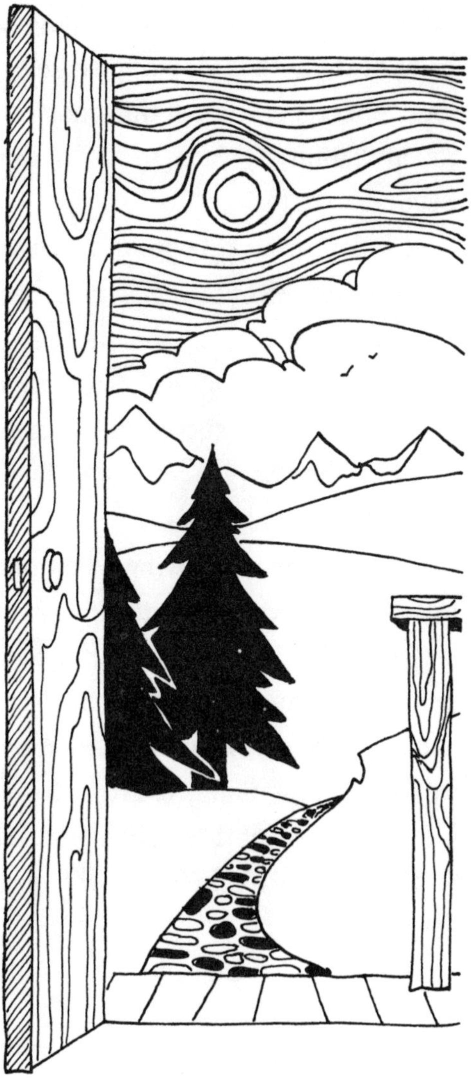

as someone else's choice for a special liturgy, someone else's superior skill. It might show up as the demand to be at peace with my own mistake or to trust another for forgiveness. Let me see this doorway as it is, and accept its invitation. I want to walk through and out and beyond.

If I stopped at this point, I would be giving a false—and perhaps discouraging—impression. Many doors have opened for me since the incident I've just described. They have swung or creaked or cracked open, and I have not always been successful in negotiating passage. In many a door have I got stuck. But better one foot out than neither, I always say.

And to keep on moving when one's exit is somewhat less than graceful, to wriggle through, fall through, or stagger out can often be as effective a departure as the perfect, determined, unhesitating step. When we have to shoulder the considerable burden of "Now I've fouled it up," our temptation is to crumple under the load. Don't. Keep going. Scramble, crawl. Just keep on going, even if you're given a black eye by the door you almost didn't get through.

Peace

I'll miss coming up here after Vigils. It's so quiet. Quiet. One of the juniors brought to class a beautiful phrase from Guerric of Igny: "the silence and secrecy of interior peace." On the one hand, it sounds like something you might try for, ask for, even be given; at least in the form God feels is best for you, safest for you. Sometimes we don't recognize what we want when we get it, because it doesn't look like what we asked for.

If interior peace had to translate into a constant and unruffled state of suspension from irritation, anxiety, concern, frustration, and exhilaration; if it meant we never had to suffer from the nonsense of self-importance or self-disgust (alternately and conjointly); if it provided exemption from reactions to failure, inadequacy, and the incompatible qualities of one's neighbor, we might correctly junk the possibility of having it. And who would want it anyway?

Interior peace means choices—choosing to turn one's head away from irritations we have no obligation to brood over; choosing to trust a God who gets romantic at the wrong time—There he is, taking our hands in his when we'd much rather leave them on the steering wheel.

Trust, I might say reluctantly enough, is everything. Trust is hope and faith, and at those moments when we determine to see in the things we most want to argue about, thrash under, and pay God back for, only a series of invitations into the wide places of his heart, it is love. Or it can be love if we ask it to be so.

◊

The Bottom of the Pedestal

My first reaction to being disapproved of is usually a good imitation of the newly caught fish flopping at the end of its line: "Get that hook OUT!" But why? What's wrong with saying you were wrong, that you brought it on yourself? And if you didn't, what's so bad about misunderstanding? People forgive. What's wrong with accepting forgiveness? People forget. It's much more restful for them to be agreeable than to nurse a grudge.

Let yourself be looked down on once in a while. The view from the bottom of the pedestal is pleasant too.

And who knows what will be happening a week from now, into what fabric today's tangled yarn will have been woven? A month and a half ago, I threw a fair tantrum over an imagined slight to my importance. All morning I boiled silently, tried to fix things and made them worse, suffered from a week's case of enflamed contrition, and saw yesterday that every trifle I objected to has fallen neatly into exactly the pattern I most wanted.

If I'd held my temper and my trust, I'd have spared myself and other people a lot of useless discomfort. If I had trusted, I would not have had anything to be mad at in the first place.

◊

The Starting Place

To start the work of conversion from the truth of God's love for me at this moment, in these circumstances, and as I now am, is not to duck out on the effort conversion demands. It's to start the effort in the right place.

A lot of Greg Louganis' skill as a diver lies in the tremendous power of his spring from the board. If our spiritual legs find strength in gratitude for an illimitable love, we'll be capable of the kind of moral effort God wants. Notice—the kind *he* wants.

We can want the wrong kind of conversion, longing to be better because we hate ourselves the way we are, or at least harbor severe reservations about God's permissive will in our regard. The work of conversion then becomes a determination to sink the self we don't appreciate. Under this emotional pressure, what God has made us capable of and the kind of conversion he wants can cease to figure in our plans. What *we* want is all that counts; and what we want is just to get away from what we are.

The radical necessity of prayer doesn't rise solely from the fact that we need grace, and grace is found in prayer. We also need to keep coming back to this starting place—the unimaginable acceptance in which God wraps us round. He runs toward us in every circumstance. He enjoys our company, smiles at our attentions and relaxes in our affection. Or, to switch the image, Christ sits ever by the well, waiting for us to come and draw, waiting to give, waiting to be comforted, not by the dream we've cooked up for tomorrow, but by the reality of today.

He wants what is possible this moment, a surrender to the privilege of being just this self instead of the one we'd rather be (and rather knock ourselves out trying to construct). From this point, he will indicate our road, a road especially built for this person he has brought so far and cherishes and has his own intentions for.

Yield to the self you are, to the plan of God unfolding slowly but steadily in the heart you feel so discontented with. Make your small plans to fit the capacity he has filled with grace, in which he waits, to which he has devoted an eternity of reverence.

You are not—truly you are not—a heap of rusty spare parts and scrap metal waiting for recycling. You are his finely-crafted masterpiece. It's easier to work at getting better if getting better is a peace treaty with the surrounding instruments of God's forming love, a willingness to see in what consoles, affirms, curtails and annoys, the desire of an eternal lover to draw us more firmly into his arms.

Much of our nastiness grows on the fallen stump of trying to be what we are not made to be. Much of our conversion grows out of the green wood of cooperation with God's idea of who we are.

◇

Helping

Some people spend their lives helping other people adjust to themselves, their neighbors, God, and the variety of perplexities attached to each. These helpers have to do their best, but part of their best is realizing how little depends on them. The people they help are not objects to be fixed, and helpers are not mechanics. Other people are not possessions, and helpers are not owners.

Those who help must learn to handle both satisfaction and failure. The emotional reaction to either can hurt or help their own growth. Failures are little deaths; so are mistakes. A helper must learn the craft of dying constructively. The craft of succeeding has more subtle requirements and adminsters its own sort of dying. Both lead to a personal experience of resurrection. One's own death and resurrection are the chief forming agents of the people one is trying to help.

I sit here listening to rain, a rain we have long needed. Now we are getting it. Lots. All the rain in the world is coming right straight down. God is coming down in waterfalls. The soil takes him in without argument.

Parable.

◇

Foothills and Floodgates

God, you are more interesting than I. You are everything beautiful, and I grow so tired of obstructing the view. May I get out of the way? Sometimes I feel as if I had hiked to the top of a hill; but from my eminence, I can see very little, for I am in my way. I am the tree that blocks the vision, the boulder I cannot climb beyond.

How restful it would be not to care about myself; how peaceful to worship in the holy place of other lives without getting nervous about the impression I am making or how I am handling the situation. I would appreciate a view of the carrot patch even, which did not feature me striking a pose along the rows. But most of all, I would like some access to you which was not dimmed and distorted by the filter of my self-involvement.

There are ways of praying which, to some extent, and

for a limited time, resolve this problem and provide the peace of not getting in the way. But that is a small part of the project. Something further is required.

The something further is an agreement to be who I am, to stop the everlasting quarrel with myself and accept the very fact of being a self, and the particular self I seem to have got stuck with. I'm not quite sure how it works, but the road to self-forgetfulness winds through the foothills of self-acceptance.

Yet I want more than this. Sometimes it seems as if the discomfort of being myself, of being a perpetual obstruction to what I want to see and love, were a very minor affliction in comparison with the pain of experiencing my solidarity with the whole of human life. Sometimes I have to slam shut emotional floodgates against a sea of horror, when the full tide of human deprivation roars up my personal beach and drags me, drowning, out to sea. This also is me. The dark waters of human history are my inheritance and my identity. History is not *they* but *I*.

I recognize in this, another quarrel with what I cannot understand, with an outcome I cannot grasp. And the way through preoccupation with this sense of collective guilt is cessation of my battle with the world.

Christ is an infinite and patient sea, absorbing and transforming the mystery of human guilt. He is the lonely gull, trumpeting eventual victory. He is the wave sloshing against a morning beach, erasing from its sand the scrawls drawn by our distorted individuality, smoothing the particular heart into peace with its own highwater mark, its harvest of clams and deserted scallop shells.

Accept yourself, accept your world. Dive into him who takes both world and self into the sea of his redemptive tenderness. Slip into the waters of his forgiving love. Accept, for a change, his way of saving.

◇

Klim

Our cat has a laconic personality. The way he regards his world is a form of instruction to anyone with the patience to learn from him. He takes his time, observes, ponders. His next move is a matter of consideration, not urgency. He waits. Nature gave him enormous beautiful eyes; they gaze.

He is currently wondering what to do next. Twice his muscles have gathered themselves together for a move, and twice they have relaxed. I avoid his eyes. Should he look up into mine, he will interpret my interest as an invitation to jump up on my desk and take a bath in the middle of all my concerns. This must not be.

Well Klim, I'm back. This little adventure is over.

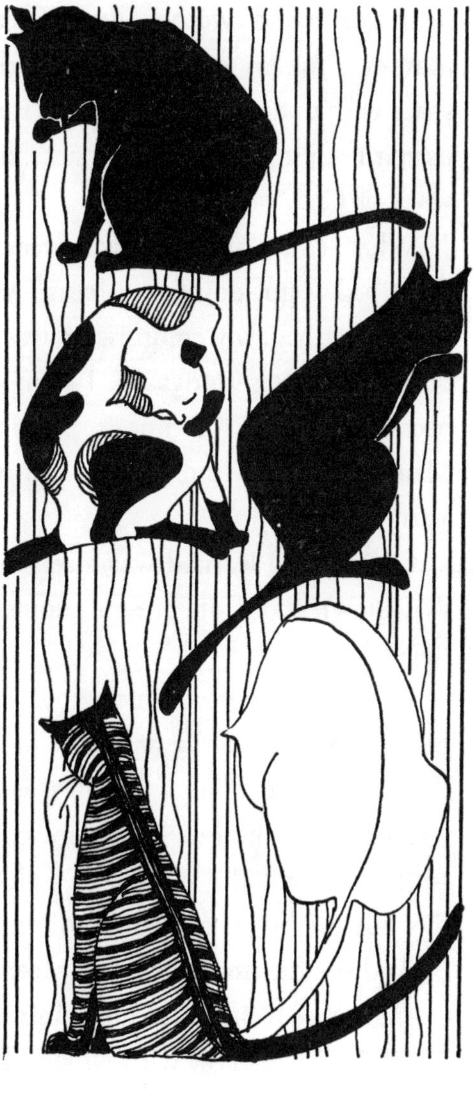

Our novitiate is a happy place and I can hardly wait for next month and two new little sisters. I'm more grateful than ever for my community and the richness it has to share with our novices; its joy and human understanding; its spirit of prayer and interior accessibility to the forming work of God.

What I've done for two weeks could be simply described as not-doing-any-harm. At least I *hope* it could be so described. My commission was not to be important but not to mess things up. I even got out of one class because we used the time to prepare a welcome for Sr. Maureen. It was fun. What I did mostly, I think, was learn.

One thing I learned was a sense of time. Yes I know I've known about the present moment for ages, but have I ever *known* it?

I do not clamor so much now after the future; I am more reconciled to the past. The ill-temper, the mistake, the impatience of ten minutes ago; the malformation wrought by a lifetime's deficient choices; the emotional contusions and the spasms of guilt—what is left of all this but the bright now of absolute forgiveness?

And the future? The future sleeps contentedly in the eternal present of an unquestioning love. The future at which I tend to claw, with which I bicker, and on which I want to fit my personally designed straight-jacket— what is it but the extension in time and matter of the eternal peace?

In this moment, rest all the difficulties and all the triumphs of all the people for whom I am concerned. This is the moment of fulfilment: Good Friday and Easter, Pentecost and the Great Return. Everything is here. The more I wander from this fullness, the weaker I am, and less helpful to the world. *Now* is everything. Now is Christ.

Klim, I consider you an image of this wholesome attitude toward time. You probe the present moment with your great and luminous eyes, sinking ever more deeply into its warm secrecy. You tell me that I have lived with insufficient reverence for the moment I am in, and that your contentment makes more sense than my agitation.

I promise to think of this whenever I run into you. I will attend your instruction with gratitude.

◊

The Dump

I can see, at the end of these reflections, that to some people I will have said exactly what I did not mean to say. They will suspect that I have been all too willing to walk off and leave the world to its misery. Concentration on hope can give the impression of pretending that the sordid and the unjust will go away if we think happy

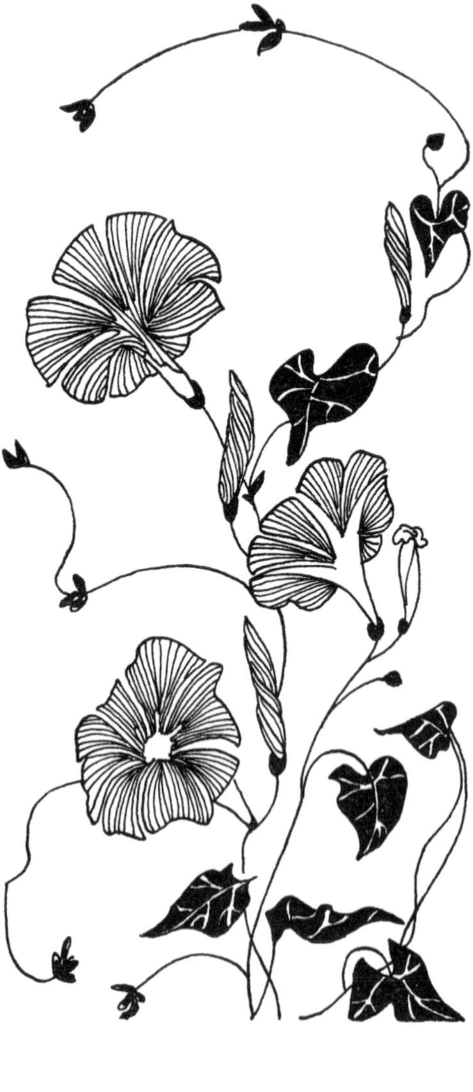

thoughts. "She is wandering in a world of her own concoction, inhabited by a God who glues broken dolls back together on rainy afternoons."

Not really.

I want to say clearly that what I am talking about is an inner attitude, an attitude which indwells and gives shape to strong practical concern for other people. It is not a substitute for the acceptance of social responsibility, but its inner life.

I have been called, myself, to a hidden form of ministry. Most people are called to extend a more visible hand to the victims of a mess we have all, unfortunately, assisted in creating. But whatever outward form it takes, our responsibility to hope is as urgent as our responsibility to extend that hope in action.

The basis of our hope is, however, the will of God, and this creates problems. Since the power of God does not leap to our whistle and work to our order, we tend to get mad. Almost worse, we tend to get edgy. This is entirely understandable. God understands bad temper even when it's directed to him. But he keeps on asking us to yield up the security of anger for the security of hope. He probably won't do things our way, but he will get them done. Confidence in eternal resolutions is not an escape from temporal responsibilities; it oils the works. Christ is not an incarnate snarl and that is not our vocation either. Hope pushes unseen boulders away from the mouths of innumerable dark caves to disclose a resurrection far more satisfying than any we could ever have projected on our own.

The pliancy given by hope can sustain blows delivered to our sense of self-esteem by people whose own sense of personal worth has been mauled by horrendous circumstances. Hope can go on loving when systems get worse instead of better and individuals show no evidence of a capacity for digging themselves out of holes. Best of all, it can respect solutions which are other, unexpected, and inexplicable; and permit the ingenuity of God to work itself out in ways that drain us of the sense of having done one darn thing to effect the improvement. Other people are not there to give us a sense of being helpful. God is not there to do what he is told.

We hope not only for the other but for ourselves; not only that the other will be gathered into the arms of God, but that we in the process of being helpful will not kick ourselves out of his embrace.

Back in our woods lies a hollow, and in that hollow lies a dump. History, in the form of maple saplings, morning glory, and a dozen species of wild greenery, has moved in on it. This collection of old car parts, tin cans, and cow bones is at the point of admitting that it is no longer a dump. On the slope nearest the path, a slim but sturdy peach tree blossoms every spring before its taller neighbors eat up its sun. It probably grew from a pit that got thrown in the dump, and it has a lot to say about hope.